Houses of Cloth

by Wendy Etzel

RCW
PUBLISHING COMPANY

PUBLISHING COMPANY

Houses of Cloth©
©1994 by Wendy Etzel
Rebecca C. Wilber Publishing Company
RR #3, Old Post Lane
Columbia Cross Roads, Pennsylvania 16914-9535
717-549-3331

ISBN 0-9627646-7-1

Thanks

I'd like to thank all those who have given so much support throughout this project:

All my quilting students and friends - for their encouragement, enthusiasm, and loyalty over the past eighteen years.

Judith Youngman - my friend and advisor, co-conspirator, sounding board, editor, ... I can't imagine completing this project without her.

Jim - my husband and friend - for believing that I should and could do whatever I wanted to. At last he will know what I've been up to!

Kirsti - my daughter - for her wonderful drawings of local houses and folding hundreds of patterns in record time.

Jay - my son - for all his computer assistance and critical observations of quilts in progress.

My Mom - for being my most enthusiastic cheerleader throughout my life.

Family - for encouraging me to continue writing my very long Christmas letters for the past 26 years and actually making their friends and neighbors read them.

Everett Rubendall, Kelly Orso, Debi Porter and the Lycoming County Museum staff - for enthusiastically searching for events that I might find interesting.

Lynn Balassone - graphics designer and layout editor - for her patience and total involvement in this project and Williamsport even when I dragged her to the Wildwood Cemetery in the rain.

Gloria Stere - Stere's Sewing Center - for all the expert advice about sewing machines and keeping me updated on all that is new on the market.

Preservation Williamsport - for their continuing efforts to protect and restore local treasures and educate those who have forgotten their value.

Eric and Nina Cheetham - owners of the Peck House (cover quilt) - congratulations for giving new life to this very special home. Few will ever imagine all that you have done.

Mark and Rebecca Wilber - publishers - for their support and commitment to this project and allowing me all the freedom that I could ever want.

Terry Wild Studios - Photographing quilts while hanging from barn beams 20 feet above the floor is no easy task. It was a pleasure to work with everyone at the studio.

About the Author

"In order to really see and appreciate what surrounds us we must step back and pretend that we are visitors looking upon a scene that we have never viewed."
Author

In 1968 after completing a graduate teaching degree at Penn State, Wendy and her husband traveled to Chile to teach school. Although much time has passed since spending those three years in a foreign culture, Wendy attributes much of her development to experiences in a country where the customs and arts of the past could be witnessed first hand. In a land where nothing is familiar the visitor begins to examine and reflect upon all that is seen.

Upon returning to the USA, the Etzels settled again in State College, PA and began raising a family. Wendy took advantage of the excellent art classes and studied painting, jewelry making, sculpture and pottery.

In 1973 the Etzel family moved to Williamsport, PA, a town rich in architecture and history. Wendy enrolled in an afternoon quilting class and swiftly buried fifty pounds of wet clay. Combining her love of teaching and quilting seemed natural and after conducting those first classes at the community college, she opened a modest studio in her basement where many a student collided with low hanging heating ducts.

Presently Wendy is teaching a wide variety of classes and helping students select fabrics from her meticulously chosen stock in a Victorian home with ten foot ceilings. Although most of her time is spent on her own fall and spring teaching schedules and focused quilters retreats, Wendy has lectured and taught classes for guilds throughout the North East. Additionally she has conducted week long workshops in Canada at the St. Lawrence Summer School of the Arts; in the fall of '92 Wendy traveled to Australia where she directed workshops, lectured, and participated in professional forums at the Australasian Quilt Conference.

A life long love of architecture, and houses in particular, has influenced Wendy's work in picture quilts. To encourage others to portray homes in their quilts, she directs workshops in which participants are guided through each phase of their fabric constructions. Her goal to bring the history of Williamsport to the public through her quilts is an ongoing challenge.

Kirsti Lyn Ettel '95

Contents

Close-up of the Herdic House quilt on page 19

List of Quilts

INTRODUCTION

Since the beginning of time man's shelters have presented us with a tangible record of the past. Having outlived their designers, builders and owners, our old houses embody far more than the brick and mortar that comprise their walls. They are symbols of a period of time, and hold all the accounts of the families that lived within their walls. Whether that home is a castle from an age far removed, or a simple white farmhouse, it is the people and their stories that give it life and a character all its own. Few of us will ever be honored with a monument or a bronze statue; however our homes will always stand to remind our friends and family of those times when laughter and love were shared.

When we as quilters decide to include a house in our quilts, we record a bit of history; perhaps it is our own, or maybe that of someone we feel should be remembered. In a way we have the opportunity to add life to our work and allow the admirer to become involved in the past.

As quiltmakers with an appreciation for color and design, and a fascination for piecing and construction, it is no wonder we are naturally drawn to houses and architecture. We are quite familiar with building techniques and their orderly sequence, and know that precision and accuracy are important. Although our materials are different, we can become two-dimensional contractors without a lengthy apprenticeship or a costly investment of materials. As a matter of fact, our houses never need to be repainted and roofs never leak.

Each house that a quilter decides to construct, presents the sewer with problems that are unique to that structure. This book is designed to give the reader direction and guidance in beginning that construction. The descriptions of the quilts printed in this book reveal the ways that unusual structural features were handled. However, with each new building comes the challenge for new solutions. If the simple steps outlined are followed, the quilter is free to concentrate on those special features which will demand attention.

In addition to the outline for housing and landscape construction, this book includes some of the history of the people whose lives were spent in the houses represented in the quilts. Perhaps these stories will lead you to look within the walls of many of the fine old homes that cross your path or simply record the history of your very own family.

I dedicate this book to all those whose architectural creations have inspired us to examine their work and the quilters who have chosen to preserve them in cloth.

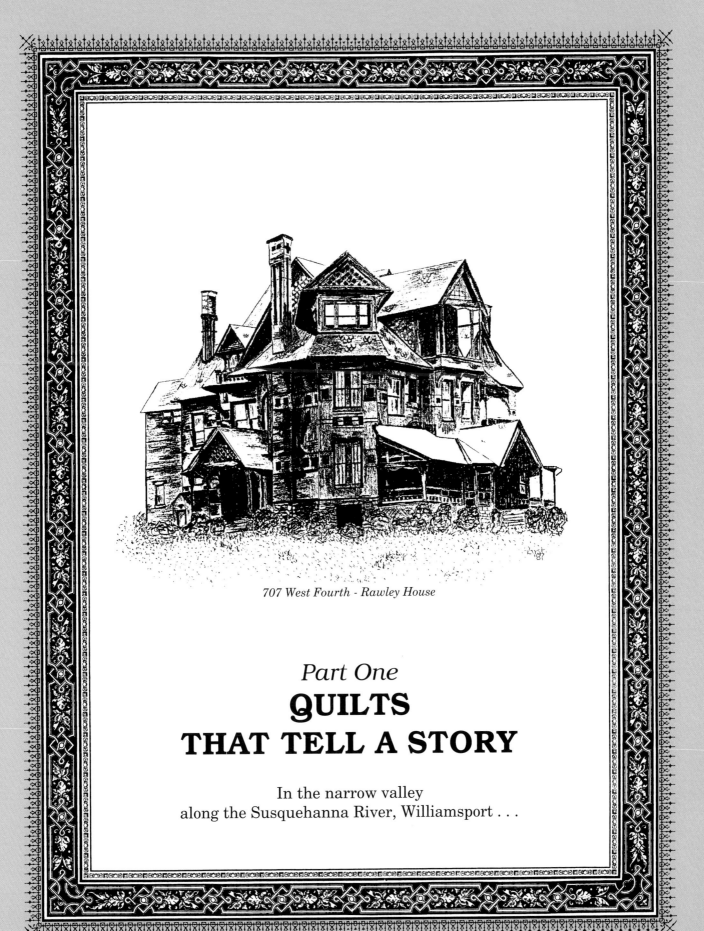

707 West Fourth - Rawley House

Part One
QUILTS
THAT TELL A STORY

In the narrow valley
along the Susquehanna River, Williamsport . . .

THE RUSSELL INN
1796 - 1871

FOURTH AND MULBERRY STREET
WILLIAMSPORT, PA

In a long, narrow valley along the Susquehanna River, Williamsport became home to settlers who found the area much like the mountainous forest land they left in Northern Europe. Early accounts of the town written in the New York Sun in 1876 said "its first settlers were Quakers and Pennsylvania Dutch. They raised cabbage, ate sauerkraut, and lived and died without excitement. Somnolent and plodding by nature, the town reflected their somnolency,.... Its growth was very slow... The only ways to reach it were by canal boat or stagecoach... This colony of Quakers and Dutchmen lay there like a nest egg, totally unconscious of the wealth in coal and timber that surrounded them..."

In 1796 James Russell, an Irishman, erected a simple log structure about two blocks from the river. The first floor was divided into four rooms and a large brick chimney ran up the middle of the building, affording a fireplace for each of the front rooms. A stairway ascended to the second floor where three rooms were used as sleeping quarters. A large garret served as a store room and sleeping apartment. The house had a shingle roof put on with handmade nails. The Russell Inn was the first house in Williamsport as well as the only place where travelers could be entertained. In its first year, it even served as the first Court House when Williamsport was designated as the county seat.

In the 75 years that the Russell Inn stood, this isolated, self-sufficient town grew into a bustling community that turned from farming to lumbering. Nearly 45 taverns now served its population of 16,000. In August of 1871, fire destroyed a several block area of the town as well as its first tavern, the Russell Inn.

Newspaper photo of first structure in Williamsport on northeast corner of East Third and Mulberry Streets

"THE RUSSELL INN"

With the picture of the Russell Inn to examine, fabrics were carefully chosen to best represent every aspect of the scene. A dark brown, parchment-like fabric was selected for the logs. A streaked, beige colored Indian dyed cotton was perfect for the chinking since it shaded from light beige to medium tans. A plaid was used for the roof and was sliced apart and resewn directly onto a paper roof template so that the lines in the plaid followed the angle of the roof. For windows, a black plaid with tan and white lines was perfect. Simple rectangles with the edges pressed under were appliqued to the structure. *Picture This,* a glue-like substance formulated to transfer photos to fabric, was used to affix the lettering to fabric for the tavern billboards. The two adjoining buildings were constructed with a wonderful striped brown fabric and the reverse side was used on the building on the right to accentuate the front face of the building. A fabric resembling stone was tea-dyed and used on both its right and wrong sides to form the building foundations. Very narrow tucks were sewn into the sidewalk fabric to give the illusion of partitions and edges. The sky was dye-painted on wet muslin and the foreground was a perfect, ground-like drapery fabric found on a remnant pile.

During construction, no actual log home drawings were made. An approximate size for the length of the house was necessary so that the strips of brown and beige in the log unit could be sewn. The finished log unit was then sliced where the inside corner for the building would be located. One side of the unit was raised so that the logs looked like they were resting on each other. In addition, the log unit on the right was positioned, as it was in the actual photo, to indicate perspective. A slice of brown log fabric covered the corner. While closely examining the photo of the Inn, newsprint shapes were folded and refolded until the desired roof or chimney shape were achieved. Fabric was then sprayed lightly with starch and ironed over the paper shape. The procedures used in the step by step building guide were then followed. When the building was complete, it was sewn to the background using nylon thread. Lastly the entire scene was machine quilted and the sky was quilted by hand.

"The Russell Inn"
(1991) - 40" x 42" - author

PETER HERDIC
A MAN WITH A VISION
1824-1888

Born in 1824, Peter Herdic was the youngest of eight children. He quickly learned about the hardships of life after his father died, leaving the family destitute. By the age of four, Peter could be found eagerly trailing his older brothers as they carried wood and preformed whatever chores they could find to help their struggling family. As the boys attended school, Peter then six, learned to write his name in the sand; the extent of his formal schooling, since his mother remarried and moved the family to a rural farm.

Always energetic and industrious, by the age of ten, Peter could cut a cord of wood in a day and in addition would frequently walk five miles to dispose of quails and rabbits that had been caught in his snares during the hours of the preceding night. It was during these years that he was greatly influenced by a neighbor

who took a fancy to young Peter. Often he would spend time telling this young lad just how he had acquired large amounts of property by honest industry , first in earning and then in saving. First and foremost Peter was told that he must never spend his wages, but must immediately lend them out at interest. All spending money must be earned by trading or by jobs outside his regular work. Secondly, one must always keep his promises and never depart from the principles of strict integrity in business.

"These familiar talks made a deep impression upon his young mind, and no doubt laid the foundation of those habits of frugality and acquisitiveness which became such ruling passions for him in afterlife."

History of Lycoming County, PA. - 1876

When about thirteen years old, Peter's stepfather died, again necessitating a family move. This time his mother sold the family farm and bought 50 acres of wild forest land. For the next seven years everyone's energies were spent clearing and cultivating the family farm. Although his mother wanted Peter to take over by the time he was twenty, he declined, leaving the farm to his brother, and set out to find employment.

In his first job, Peter commenced work at a sawmill on Thursday, and by Saturday, had gained one additional day by working two extra half-days. By Monday, Peter was promoted to the "head of the gate", fixing his wages at 75 cents per day and board, the highest wage paid to the best men. After a year Peter collected all the wages owed to him and joined the working crew at another sawmill for $12 per month and board. The money he received from his first job was loaned to his new employer at 7% interest. After 6 months, Peter had $60 coming to him, having spent $12 for clothing. This $60 was also loaned back to his employer at the same interest rate. This cycle of hard work, frugality and investment, continued and in three years, Herdic had $383 of invested income earning 7% interest. Outside operations such as trading in sheep and piling boards at the mill yielded him sufficient funds for every day expenses.

By now Mr. Herdic was almost twenty -three years old and ready to enter the world of business. With a partner, his first purchase was that of a mill that produced shingles. After only three years, both owners had accumulated assets worth about $2,500. At last Peter felt more settled and able to become the head of a household. In 1849, at the age of twenty -five, he bought a farm north of Williamsport and married.

Central part of Williamsport in 1840.

In the year following his marriage, Peter purchased a large tract of pine timber and erected his first sawmill. Dense white pine and hemlock forests with canopies so high that trees rose more than 100 feet before bearing branches, covered the area. Ship builders from Boston to Baltimore depended on the white pine for clipper ships' masts and spars. Mr. Herdic's purchases of timber lands, as well as the sale of his saw mill, yielded him huge profits.

Quiet farm life, once so attractive, was no longer venerated, and in the fall of 1853, at the age of twenty-nine, Peter Herdic came to Williamsport. After his arrival, he systematically began to purchase large tracts of land that bounded the western edge of the city (Hepburn St.). In this pursuit, he would spend more than $300,000, an enormous sum for these times, over the next twelve years. His visions of a grand city began to unfold as the lumber industry boomed. After building and operating a flour mill for a short time, Peter returned to the more attractive lumber business. At age thirty-three, Peter became a partner in the Susquehanna Boom Company, the operators of a crib-like holding area for logs headed for the mills. Through the collection of tolls placed upon the logs, the partners became millionaires in a very short time. In addition to holdings in extensive sawmills, he soon became a part of every aspect of this growing town, establishing its banks, newspa-

pers, gas works, opera house, churches, a grand hotel, and hundreds of homes for both the rich and the poor. Never having had the advantage of a formal education, he kept all these transactions in his head.

Peter Herdic's wife died not long after his appearance in Williamsport, and by now, he felt the need to become a part of the society his wealth had afforded him. In addition to taking lessons on the finer graces of life, he married the daughter of a prestigious judge. His new wife, Encie, was one of the most elegant, brilliant, and accomplished of her sex. Their mansion, built soon after coming to Williamsport in 1855, was the finest in the city. In these early days, elaborate homes began to arise along dusty, dirt roads and

Peter Herdic's home at 405 W. Fourth St. - 1994

coexisted amidst rough-and-tumble logging camps.

As the lumber industry thrived, so did the city. In 1865 Peter opened the Herdic House, a grand , 4-story hotel about a mile from the center of the city. Rooms for entertaining 700 guests boasted the finest materials from around the world. As a matter of fact, Herdic forbade the architect to tell him of any of the costs while construction was underway. When complete, the hotel was surrounded by a deer park and a special horse-drawn carriage was available to carry guests to the center of town free of charge. The final tally for the construction reached $225,000, a price far above the cost of an elaborate Victorian home which ran no more than $4,000 during this time period.

Just four years after opening the finest hotel on the East coast, Herdic became infatuated with the idea of a health retreat located forty miles to the north of Williamsport in Canton. As with most of his conceptions, a small frame cabin beside a natural spring, quickly grew into a full scale resort. Before it succumbed to fire, Minnequa, as it was called, became one of the famous haunts for the wealthy seeking health and pleasure.

Herdic's unbounded energy and faith in his own abilities led him into every facet of city life. Instead of husbanding his capital, he was stimulated to wild speculation and often involved the city council in undertaking projects which he felt strongly about. Huge debts began to accumulate, and as the mayor in 1870, Herdic signed bonds to fund the construction of sewer systems, roads, and bridges. In order to display his commitment to the city, Herdic himself bought and resold the bonds guaranteeing their interest and payments.

At a time when it was thought impossible for him to withstand the financial pressures, Herdic commissioned the building of an impressive, Gothic style Episcopal church at a cost of $80,000, $50,000 over its original esti-

Trinity Episcopal Church

mate. After outrage was expressed, Herdic decided to personally pay for the church and proceed with his next endeavor, a full block of 5-story brick buildings which included an opera house. Borrowed money was used for his latest construction and his vast business dealings were now a network of liens, mortgages, and endorsements.

By 1878 the depression had struck and at the age of fifty-four, Peter Herdic was bankrupt. No one knew how such a man could have accumulated 2 million dollars of debt. As Herdic left the city to escape from his many creditors, his vast collection of properties, as well as his elegant household furnishings, were sold by the local sheriff.

...20 acres with brick house, barn and tobacco sheds to John Reading for $50... coal lands in Pine township, 3000 acres for $25... The grand Herdic House Hotel for $1,200... the 5-story business block (still incomplete) for $50... 12 city properties for $50 to $10.

Most men would have been defeated by the enormity of this crash; however, Herdic, a true financial wizard, virtually lived in the future and was already working on his next ventures. By 1880 he was moving along with the manufacture of the "herdic", a light weight horse drawn carriage designed to carry passengers for a fare of 10 cents. Peter himself held the patent for the design and several cities in the state invested in his carriages to commence their public transportation needs.

In addition to projects in other cities, plans were underway for transforming 80 acres of farmland, laying to the northwest of Williamsport, into a planned community. Charters for a water works, steam heating plant, gas and electric light works were all secured and were to operate from one center for the benefit of all. Large numbers of dwellings which would be rented for $10 a month or sold outright, were to be constructed, affording better and cheaper housing through such large

wholesale building. The estimated cost of this giant undertaking was placed at $1,000,000.

In February of 1888, while inspecting his water works system in Huntington, PA., Peter fell and fractured his skull. Refusing to see a doctor, he pressed on for several weeks until his condition worsened. When doctors in New York City were finally summoned, they could not understand how he had lived in a rational state after such a severe injury. Evidently they didn't know Peter Herdic as the people of Williamsport did. They had no idea that he had a most wonderful brain. Peter Herdic's death at age sixty-four, marked the passing of one of the most colorful and significant characters in Williamsport.

Had Peter Herdic lived longer, it is believed he would surely have become a very wealthy individual again; and the parcels of land recorded in the records under his name, would extend beyond the 630 already listed.

Peter Herdic gave his name to the English language with his invention of a
public transportation conveyance. Dictionaries today list it like this:
"herdic (after Peter Herdic, Amer. inventor): a small horsedrawn omnibus of
late 19th century America having side seats and an entrance at the back."

"AN AFTERNOON AT THE PETER HERDIC HOUSE"

In recent years the residence of Peter Herdic has been given new life. For decades it had been abused and neglected as tenants simply used its space without any reverence to its original owner. Now this wonderfully elaborate home serves as a fine restaurant where patrons can dine in the parlors once used by the man who changed the course of this city. What a perfect beginning for a quilt!

I have always felt that the presence of people in any painting or photo adds to the interest of the composition. In order to find the proper setting for the Herdic house, I searched through old photos taken during the late 1800's and finally, paintings by the masters. When I came upon Winslow Homer's painting, "The Croquet Players", I looked no further.

With photos of the Herdic house to study, a drawing was made on graph paper. The soft pink fabric chosen for the exterior best represented the actual color. In order to add depth, pieces of the pink were tea-dyed in two darker shades to be used for the shaded areas of the house. A delicate cream colored print was used for the curtains and a soft black selected for the interior of the house. The unusual trim, carved bracketed eaves and ornate window moldings, presented a real problem. After searching for laces and trims for months, a student suggested I simply have someone crochet what I wanted. In a matter of days a friend had done just that. The house was assembled and sewn in three sections following the steps outlined.

Next a very general sketch indicating the house and tree with the shadow was drawn in its actual size. The simple shapes were then outlined with black marker and served as a guide (placed under a sheet of plastic) when it was time to dye paint the grass. Because of the large size of the finished quilt the sky and the grass portions were painted separately. Both the sky and lawn each began with the soaking of a 2 yard length of muslin in a solution of sodium carbonate. After drying and ironing, the pieces were stretched over plastic on my work table and secured with clothes pins. The sky area was sprayed with water and then painted. The grass area was also dampened slightly and green dyes were sponged on with pieces of a natural sponge. Since my drawing indicating the tree and people shadows could be seen through the muslin, those areas were painted more heavily. After allowing both to dry, I was not satisfied with the intensity of the grass portion. I soaked the 2 yards again in sodium carbonate and repainted, adding more depth to the lawn. I also dyed an extra half yard of both sky and lawn to be used as a base for sewing trees onto. Lastly, the sky and lawn portions were seamed

"An Afternoon at the Peter Herdic House"
(1991) - 74" x 67" - author
Best of Show - QBL - 1991

together and tacked to a styrofoam board creating the working wall upon which the design was built.

In constructing each of the trees, I felt it was important that the sky fabric be seen through the leaves. First I seamed a piece of sky and grass fabric together forming a rectangle upon which I could construct my tree. (See landscape chapter) After the trees were completed they were pinned to the scene and bushes added. One by one, the trees, bushes, and sections of the flower gardens were placed and moved until the completed landscape was composed. Where many small bushes overlapped and touched each other, they were carefully pinned and then stitched together forming a section of the landscape that could be handled more easily. Nothing was attached to the background at this time however. The Victorian ladies and one fine gentleman were constructed and their separate sections were hand sewn together and set aside until the game was ready to be played.

Although this may seem like a step backwards, I realized that if I wanted to quilt the grass in a stippling fashion, I would run into trouble when I encountered a bush or, worse yet, a lady playing croquet. Because of this, I removed all the shrub sections and trees, as well as the house, and sandwiched the background sky and lawn with cotton batting and the fabric for the back of the quilt, pinned the 3 layers together, and machine quilted the entire lawn section using fine smoke- colored nylon thread. In the sky portion, I hand quilted cloud and wind current shapes. Since I planned on adding a border to my quilt, I allowed extra batting and backing to extend beyond the sky and lawn sections.

Now it was time to replace the house, trees, and people. Each was carefully pinned to the quilted background and either appliqued by hand or by machine, using a hem or pin stitch and nylon thread. Since many of these elements were large, they then needed to be machine quilted so that they blended into the heavily quilted background. By this time the quilt was much more awkward to handle and the people were hand-sewn to the lawn and a little bit of hand quilting was added to enhance their clothing.

Lastly , the borders were added and then quilted with gold metallic thread. In trying to simulate the look of an antique frame, I decided to stitch a chain of daisies along the inner edge of the striped, black border with the gold thread. The gold band created the beaded look I wanted. It was difficult, however, to control the decorative stitches along such a long line while sewing through all three layers. In addition, the tight stitches did have a tendency to shorten the border length slightly. After the sleeve and binding was added, a sigh of relief was expelled.

THE PECK HOUSE
1872

1075 WEST 4TH STREET
WILLIAMSPORT, PA.

Williamsport's prosperity peaked in the 1880's. Its thirty sawmills had turned nearly 32 million logs into lumber and the city could boast about having more millionaires per capita than any other city in the world - 18 out of 19,000. With Peter Herdic's purchase of land and the development of streets to the west of the city, West Fourth Street truly became "Millionaires Row". Mansions were set back from the street where their beauty could be viewed and possibly envied. During this period it was customary to show the extent of one's wealth and fierce competition among the newly rich produced architectural creations found in few areas.

During those old-fashioned winters, it usually started snowing about the first of December and often continued until the first of April. Six foot mounds of snow remained as horse-drawn plows merely pushed it aside, enabling the "Black Marias" to be brought out. These horse-drawn carriages, covered with black oil cloth, had bobsled runners, long side seats, and floors covered with straw to help keep passengers warm. On an occasional cold evening, the tinkling of bells told that sleighs were busily engaged in gathering up all the costumed ladies and gentlemen who were off to the Herdic House, now the grandest hotel in Pennsylvania . Once inside, the winter winds were quickly forgotten as the sweet sound of music and the heavenly aromas from the warm ovens filled the air.

Near the western end of West Fourth Street, Darius Peck constructed one of the most aesthetic, Gothic style mansions on the street in 1872. From any angle one could admire the elaborate porches, gently sloping roofs, and tall elegant windows. Mr. Peck was among those involved in the booming lumber business.

He came to Williamsport to be near his business partners as well as to establish his young daughters in an area where very wealthy husbands might fit into their futures.

After only four years of residence in their new home, tragedy struck when both the Peck's young daughters were claimed by the diphtheria epidemic of 1876. Josie who was eight and Katie nine, died on the same day in March. Thirteen young children on this short stretch of Fourth Street were also lost that spring. The couple never had any other children of their own but had great affection for a niece who later came to live with them after her own marriage.

After sitting vacant and forlorn for years, the Peck house is being given new life as its current owners are actively engaged in restoring this fine old mansion. Fortunately, the original white marble fireplace, ornately carved plaster ceilings, and elaborate 10 ft. mirrors are still intact and will again grace this truly magnificent structure.

Inscription on grave markers:
Josie
Born October 26, 1869
Died March 16, 1876
*He shall Gather the
Lambs in his arms*

Katie
Born February 24, 1867
Died March 16, 1876
*And carry them
in his Bosom.*

The Peck House is wearing a new coat of paint for the winter of '94.

"A VICTORIAN WINTER IN 1872"

While browsing in a local gallery two years ago, I found myself captivated by a beautifully framed print that featured a stark white house nestled in snow. The house resembled many of the old mansions here in town and its image of winter's white elegance haunted me for months. I returned to the gallery and purchased the print of the original oil painting entitled "Victorian Winter" by Richard Schmidt. The challenge had presented itself - white house, white trim, white curtains, white snow, bare trees. I rarely work in light colors and had no idea how I would manage to achieve the soft, delicate image envisioned in my head.

Choosing an appropriate structure was not difficult. The Peck house had captured my imagination since arriving here in Williamsport. Sitting vacant for years, its graying paint and sagging porches broadcast its deteriorating condition; however, a more conscious gaze unveiled the beauty of it's silhouette as well as the extraordinary details that embellished its framework. Obviously the skilled architect designing the structure placed no bounds on his imagination.

After photographing the house and examining newspaper photos printed at a time when the house was to be demolished, a drawing was made. As an experiment, I thought I would attempt to use an overhead projector to focus my photograph onto a large sheet of graph paper taped to a wall. I sketched the house outline including windows, porch lines, etc. Because of the angle at which the original photo was taken, I then needed to redraw some of the lines and level the windows. The technique of using the overhead projector is worth a try, although it is not a cure-all to drawing difficulties. When it was time to make a second copy of the drawing, the house was divided into two vertical sections. This later made turning and sewing under the arm of the machine far easier.

A very light gray fabric was chosen for the house exterior. On the left portion of the house, the right side was used and on the section of the house that sets further back, the reverse or wrong side of the gray was used to give a slightly shaded appearance. A white cotton with white flowers was chosen for curtains and a dark, marble-like fabric selected to represent the interior of the house.

As actual sewing began, the steps outlined in the chapter on construction were followed. When approaching the windows, the side and lower trims were constructed as you would the

"A Victorian Winter in 1872"
(1992) - 49" x 60" - author

appliqued stem of a flower. Bias bars were utilized in the ironing process. When these were sewn to the structure, a strip of white yarn was slipped underneath to give an added dimension. The raw edges on the sill were simply tucked under as they were top stitched. In tackling the elaborate moldings decorating the top of the windows, I chose to form the heavy arch as a lined facing. A template was cut and traced onto thin white organdy. This outline was laid on top of the gray cotton and the pencil line served as a guide for a sewing line. After trimming, a slit was made in the organdy and the entire shape was turned inside out. Since the actual house moldings are not flat, pieces of string were slipped into the molding and secured when they were attached to the house using a zipper foot.

After the house was complete, snow was painted onto the roof with fabric paint. In examining the windows, I decided that the curtains appeared too flat and uniform. After practicing on scraps, I brushed some water onto each curtain and then added a diluted mix of blue dye paint. This same mix was also used to accent the area of the house that was recessed. Adding any paint to a completed house is quite unnerving, however, the results can take your fabric applique into the arena of the painter where shadows add depth and reality. At times it is worth the risk not to "play it safe".

In beginning the landscape, a purchased yard of dye-painted sky was sewn to the fabric I chose for the foreground, a cotton with bold strokes of white, beige, blue and tan. With the house pinned onto this large rectangle, portions of lace were draped, folded, and layered allowing the underlying snow fabric to show through. In the foreground, a piece of white silk was slipped underneath a piece of white lace with a silver metallic design.

The trees and shrubs and the fence were sewn on the machine using dissolving interfacing (Solvy by Sulky) and fine white bridal netting. Pieces of lace were sandwiched between the layers to achieve the look of snow. This method is described in the landscape section.

After the placement of the trees and snow mounds were finalized, a layer of cotton batting and a backing were slipped under the sky and foreground fabric. The house and surrounding trees were pinned and machine quilted using free motion techniques. Lastly, the sky portion of the quilt was actually" tied" by using a single snow flake motif on the Pfaff. Just a few clear beads were added to create a hint of sparkle. After completing the sky portion, I thought about the possibility of using actual constellation formations as a quilting design. Along the upper edge I found just enough space to add the Big Dipper in its local winter location.

Since heavy machine quilting often distorts the outside edge of a quilt, I chose to add the borders after the entire fabric picture was quilted. A thin burgundy strip was chosen to frame the quilt and white borders and binding completed the wintry scene. After attaching the white borders, I inserted a tuck by folding each white strip in half, toward the burgundy strip, and seaming along the fold on the wrong side. The wide white border was now quilted without any visible machine stitches.

Reprinted from the Daily Gazette & Bulletin - circa 1874

AN EVENING AT THE HERDIC HOUSE

GRAND FULL DRESS ASSEMBLY

Gay Scenes at the Herdic House - Youth, Beauty, Wealth and Fashion - The Light, Fantastic Toe - The Ladies Present and the Dresses they Wore - Gentlemen in Attendance - Full Particulars

The full dress Grand Assembly at the Herdic House last night was the most brilliant ever seen in Williamsport, and will long be held in remembrance by those who had the good fortune to be present, on account of the pleasures enjoyed, and the magnificent appearance of the dancing room, the elegance of the toilettes of the ladies, and all that was calculated to add to the enjoyment of the evening. It was gotten up expressly as a compliment to Messrs. Scofield and Barry, those gentlemen who have earned such a good reputation on account of their successful management of this great hotel, by their friends. The young men under whose auspices the affair was brought about labored with untiring industry from day to day to make it in every sense an ovation to the proprietors of the house, and one that should reflect the highest credit on all concerned. That they were completely successful none will question, who had the pleasure of being present on the occasion, and mingled in the festivities, witnessed the gorgeous scenes in the reception and dancing room, where, age, youth and beauty blended in one harmonious whole, only content upon having as much enjoyment as the occasion would afford.

THE RECEPTION

As early as 8 o'clock in the evening all was bustle and activity in the great hotel. The magnificent parlors were in a blaze of resplendent light, and servants flitted hither and thither as the hour for the reception drew near. The most perfect order prevailed. The merry tinkling of bells on the streets told that sleighs were busily engaged in gathering up the ladies who were to participate in the festivities of the evening. On the arrival of guests, they were politely directed to the dressing rooms above by servants stationed at suitable points in the halls.

Everything being in readiness the doors of the great parlors were thrown open about 9 o'clock and the proprietors, with their ladies, took their station. A band of music in the south front discoursed sweetly as the guests made their appearance, and were presented by T. L. Case, Esq., who did the honors with a dignity entirely free from all conventionality. They were received with cordial grasp and hearty shake of the hand, which at once relieved them of all diffidence, and made them feel at home without further ceremony.

As the spacious parlors filled up, the scene was an animated one - the ladies, in their beautiful costumes, as they promenaded up and down, were the entire attraction.

Col. Starkweather, one of the managers of the dancing room, was in his element and went through the different ceremonies with the ardor and vivacity of early youth. Buoyant hope beamed from his genial countenance - a man of large heart, the friend of the young, he had a smile for all.

After a few minutes spent in pleasant conversation the procession formed and marched to...

THE DANCING HALL

This was in the spacious dining room on the west end of the building. Three great chandeliers shed a flood of brilliant light upon the gorgeous scene about to open. The music struck up, the grand march took place, and soon the devotees of Terpsichore paid homage at her shrine. The magnificent dresses of the ladies, some trailing in negligent splendor, displayed their charms to the greatest advantage, as they joined in the revelry of the dance.

THE MUSIC

Repas full brass band furnished the reception and promenade music under the direction of its veteran leader. The dancing music was furnished by Prof. Singerhoof's fine string band, which was all that could be desired. The fairy like feet of the ladies kept time to the quick notes as they gracefully flitted through the intricacies of the mazy dance, and with beaming smiles of delight added enjoyment to the occasion.

LADIES PRESENT
HOW THEY WERE DRESSED

Mrs. D. H. Merriman wore cherry tarlatan, trimmed with black lace.

Mrs. Merritt, lavender silk, trimmed with lace.

Miss Nichols, Norfolk, Va., corn colored crepe, trimmed with black velvet.

Miss Taylor, white, with scarlet silk overdress, trimmed with lace.

Miss Noyes, blue satin, white tulle overdress.

Miss Smith, green silk, black lace overdress.

Mrs. Dietrick, white, trimmed in pink.

Miss Carrie Dietrick, white alpaca, trimmed with scarlet.

Miss McManigal, white with blue. Her sister Aggie, white with pink.

Miss Alice Shaw, white, trimmed with blue velvet.

Miss Carrie Shaw, Lock Haven, white with blue trim.

Miss Belle Young, white with pink silk ruffles.

Mrs. Barry, white, trimmed with pink.

Mrs. Elliot, corn colored silk, elegantly trimmed.

Mrs. Roth, green tarlatan.

Mrs. Potter, white, richly trimmed with lavender lace

Mrs. Jordan, purple satin, velvet overdress.

Mrs. Scofield, elegant black silk, with Swiss overdress festooned with flowers.

Mrs. Dr. Alba, lavender moire antique, trimmed with black thread lace.

Mrs. Case, white, trimmed with black velvet.

Mrs. Gibson, blue silk trimmed with velvet and white lace.

Miss Huling, blue tarlatan, looped with flowers.

Miss Bell Staver, Jersey Shore, white trimmed with pink.

Miss Caldwell, corn color, trimmed with black lace and looped with flowers.

Mrs. Colton, striped silk, trimmed with black velvet.

Miss Jordan, black silk, with white overdress.

Miss Webb, Orange county, N.Y., black silk, with white overdress.

Mrs. H. White, black silk handsomely trimmed with velvet.

Mrs. McLean, white over blue - made a fine appearance.

Mrs. Munson, black silk handsomely trimmed.

Mrs. Barrows, lavender, trimmed with white.

Mrs. Starkweather, plain black silk handsomely trimmed.

Miss Walker, Mass., brown silk richly trimmed with velvet.

Miss May Smith, blue with white overdress.

Miss Emma Jones, blue silk, with white trimmings.

Miss Libby Jones, white alpaca, beautifully trimmed.

Miss Sailor, white tarlatan, with handsome pink sash.

Mrs. Hepburn, white alpaca, trimmed with black.

Miss Linn, white, with green overdress.

Miss Kinyon, white, with pink satin waist

Miss Hill, white tarlatan and pink.

Mrs. Fay, black, trimmed with black and white fringe.

Miss McCormick, elegant white and blue.

Miss Flora Foresman, very neatly and handsomely attired.

Miss Annie Campbell, white trimmed with green.

Miss Anthony, white, with blue silk trimmings.

Miss Barrett, Lewisburg, buff tarlatan, puffed, with blue sash.

Miss Kapp, Northumberland, Nile green silk, with white overskirt. Hair trimmed with flowers.

Miss Kneass, Northumberland, white dress en train, black lace shawl, hair trimmed with flowers.

*Note: Tarlatan is a thin, open-mesh transparent muslin, slightly stiffened and often coarse.

Gentlemen Present

Among the large number of gentlemen present we noticed the following:
S. D. Barrows, J. Webb, C. F. Ranstead,... W. E. Hepburn, James Linn, D. T. Mahaffey,... Jas F. Herdic,... Gen. Jordan, Harrisburg,... Dr. E. M. Alba, F. C. Herdic,...Mayor Perkins,...

The Supper

Dancing was kept up until 12 o'clock, when an intermission took place for supper, which was served in the large room to the right, as you enter the hotel South. The table, which was set in the form of a cross, literally groaned beneath the load of choice viands which it contained. The ladies were seated around the room, furnished with a napkin by the servants, and helped from the table by those having them in charge. Of course everything was provided that the most fastidious appetite could desire. The elegant and tasteful manner in which the table was decorated called forth the admiration of all. It was arranged under the superintendency of Capt. Enoch Emery, an old attache of the house, well known to the public.

Close Of The Entertainment

Refreshments being over, all hands returned to the hall and dancing was immediately resumed. The music resounded in dulcet strains of exquisite harmony, and fairy feet tripped the floor until a late hour of the night, when the Grand Assembly closed. As the sweet strains of music died away, and the wearied musicians gathered up their instruments, many couples lingered in the spacious room as if loth to leave the place where they so joyously mingled in "tripping the light fantastic toe," and basked in the smiles of friends and companions. For the pleasures of the evening and the charming entertainment, the guests were indebted to the different committees who labored with persevering industry to insure suc-

cess; and that success, complete in all its details, crowned their efforts, none will deny. The best of good feeling and harmony prevailed throughout the evening. It was the finest entertainment of the kind ever seen in Williamsport. Messrs. Scofield and Barry and their excellent ladies will long remember with pride the magnificent ovation of which they were made the recipients by their friends, and the reputation of the Herdic House, that surpassingly grand and magnificent hotel of Northern Pennsylvania, stands higher than ever.

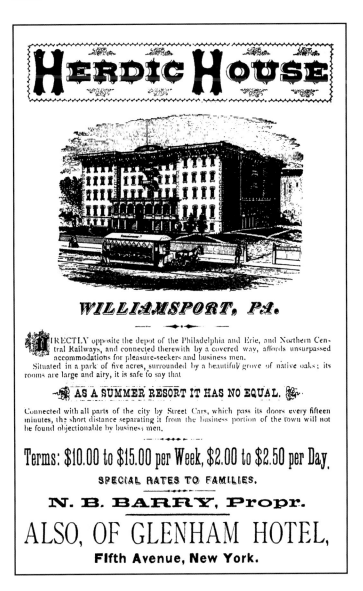

"OFF TO THE BALL" - The Ladies Present

The Herdic House, now called the Park Home, still stands in a grove of oaks in the center of Williamsport's historic district. It's fine furnishings, spectacular crystal chandeliers, and impressive oil paintings invite any visitor to step back in time. No longer a bustling hotel, it is presently a home for retired women who dine in the very ballroom where many of their ancestors once stood.

The article describing the ball was handed to me by a museum volunteer that knew I would find it fascinating. The desire to construct a "Ball" quilt was immediate although the probability of completing it before I too was ready to join the ladies at the Park Home was questionable. Fortunately, my class entitled, Off to the Ball, drew so many interested quilting students that the ballroom could be filled. The workshop was described as a day of therapy and playing with dolls. With the scraps of prom dresses and stacks of Victorian paper doll books, students designed costumes and traced shapes onto thin interfacing in their preparation of making faced applique ladies. Faces were eventually drawn with a fine permanent marker and hair was cut from a piece of fabric that featured an assortment of furry cats. By the end of the day each individual had to assess the therapeutic value of this venture into the past. It's always great fun to sew and chat with friends, although I know several eager participants would rather not "play with dolls" again.

"Off to the Ball" - (1994) - 58" x 43" - Wendy & Friends
Quilters who came to the "Ball" - Veronica Jones, Brenda Meyers, Doris Blair, Marian Gamble, Carolyn Forster, Jeanne Taylor, Evelyn Updegraff, Debbi Smith, Nancy Hepburn, Gloria Burns, Barbara Rexer, Joanne Huling, Louise Stemphle, Mary Heister, Artie Strausser, Sandy Butters, Barbara Ertel.

"600 PINE STREET"

620, 618, 614 Pine Street

"600 Pine Street" is a rendering of three wonderful little houses built in the 1880's. Immense wealth and growth drew legions of craftsmen to this new frontier in Central Pennsylvania where their creative talents and skills were in demand. Although this parcel of three houses measures a mere 84 feet in width, their unique features and elaborate trims showcase the masterful craftsmanship executed by their builders. One can only surmise that these homes were constructed by the very men that spent long hours erecting the grandiose Fourth Street mansions just a few blocks away. Although the scale was much smaller, a bit of Victorian fashion slipped into many of the working class neighborhoods.

"600 Pine Street"
(1985) - 36" x 35"
author

THE MANSION AT 1005 WEST FOURTH STREET

1869 Tax Information

John Goodrich - grocer and partner in a timber mill

Assessed value	
House (1005) -	$3,000
2 Horses -	100
1 cow -	12
Goldwatch -	50
1 Buggy -	50
Occupation-	100
	$3,312

County Tax -	$33.12
State Tax -	$ 1.83

In the mid 1860's Peter Herdic was forging ahead in his development to the West end of Fourth St. where his elegant hotel stood. With two of his partners, several grand mansions were constructed for those whose newly found riches would certainly create a market.

In true Victorian fashion the mansion at 1005 W. Fourth St. was built to proclaim the wealth of its owner. For $5,000 it was purchased by John Goodrich, a wholesale grocer, in 1869.

After eight years in residence, Goodrich found his wealth stripped away as the crash of 1877 touched many of his associates. His grand

Woman Midas Expires; Once of Williamsport

PHILADELPHIA'S wealthiest woman, Mrs. Anne Weightman Walker Penfield, 88 years old who was once a resident of Williamsport and a holder of considerable real estate in this city, died Thursday night in her Fifth Avenue apartment, New York City.

Mrs. Pennfield, whose personal fortune was estimated at more than $60,000,000, was known for many years as Philadelphia's richest woman. After the death of Hetty Green, she was generally considered the wealthiest woman in the United States.

She survived two husbands, Congressman Robert J. C. Walker and Frederick Courtland Penfield, who was American ambassador to Austria-Hungary from 1913 until the entrance of this country into the World War.

In 1862, when 18 years old, Anne Weightman married Robert J. C. Walker, a young lawyer recently graduated from Harvard. The couple moved to Williamsport in 1878 to take charge of the Weightman interests here. Walker was elected to Congress. They had one son who died while he was a college student.

The Walkers moved back to Philadelphia in 1895, Mr. Walker being taken into the firm. He died in 1903, his interests being inherited by his widow.

The following year William Weightman died, bequeathing his entire holdings to his daughter, Anne Weightman Walker, who was his sole surviving child.

Out of this will grew an action by Mrs. Jones Wister, who had been the wife of William Weightman, Jr. Mrs. Wister charged undue influence by Mrs. Walker and attempted to break the will to secure a share for her children.

In 1930, Mrs. Penfield attempted to recover federal taxes paid on her income on the grounds she had suffered heavy loss through the closing of hotel bars as a result of prohibition. Among the six hotels she owned was the Park Hotel, in Williamsport.

house was sold at a sheriff's sale for a mere $1,498.28.

Excerpts from local newspapers:

...August 3, 1878, Daily Gazette & Bulletin, Saturday Petitions in Bankruptcy filed in Pittsburgh during the past two days from the company of:
- Tabor and Goodrich -
    Williamsport - debts of $16,000
    belong to the firm
- Goodrich - debts of $14,000
- Tabor - debts of $4,000
- Peter Herdic -
    Williamsport - liabilities estimated at $3,000,000. There are 2,000 creditors on the petition.

Within the next five months the "1005" mansion was resold twice, first for $9,100 and lastly for $15,000.

At last this stately mansion had a proud new owner. Anne Weightman Walker was sent from Philadelphia to Williamsport so that her husband, a Harvard lawyer, could take charge of his Father-in-Law's vast interests acquired after Peter Herdic's bankruptcy. Anne would now oversee the splendid Herdic Hotel, purchased by her father for a mere $1,200 at sheriff sale. After changing its name to the Park Hotel, scores of carpenters, painters, plumbers and paper hangers were brought in to overhaul every room until it expressed the refined tastes of its new owner. With ten thousand rolls of wall paper, much of it gilded in gold, the improvements cost well over $20,000. For over a dozen years the Walker's lived on Fourth Street and entertained guests in grandiose style at both their home and their prestigious hotel.

After the Walker's return to Philadelphia the house was sold to J. Henry Cochran for $25,000 in 1895. In addition to his many business dealings in the lumber industry and the railroad, Cochran became a prominent State Senator. Locally he was known as the "Iceman of Fourth Street" because of his anonymous deliveries of ice to the poor. The Senator and his wife were the last to enjoy the entirety of this majestic mansion with its fourteen foot ceilings and lavish adornments.

In 1936 "1005" was sold and converted into nine apartments. Its present owners have carefully maintained this proud structure and preserved as much of its original integrity as possible.

West Fourth Street and
Trinity Church

"CRAZY QUILT MANSION AT 1005"

Creating a "Crazy Quilt" background seemed perfectly appropriate for the ornate Victorian with its wide verandas and soaring tower that I had chosen to capture in cloth. I'm sure Anne Weightman would have liked the idea; however she would have insisted on using the finest of satins and velvets and would never have imagined the addition of decorative stitches produced by machine.

Only a portion of the "1005" mansion was chosen to be represented in this particular quilt. A photo taken during the time when J. H. Cochran was in residence caught my attention as it featured a rounded side porch and a central tower. After struggling a bit with my drawing, I hopped into the car and drove off for a closer inspection. The house is now shrouded in hemlocks and few pedestrians ever notice its grandeur. The porch I was focusing on is missing entirely. In the section of the house portrayed, four different window designs were evident. In addition the surface of the building was composed of a series of towerlike structures that would have to be replicated. Fortunately a museum volunteer came upon a pen and ink drawing of the residence completed at an earlier date before the side porch was added. The artist had captured all those corners and shaded the faces of the building. By examining this very clear drawing it was possible to designate lights, darks and mediums to specific sections of the building giving the illusion of depth.

With fiber-reactive dyes and eight buckets, I dyed 1/3 yard pieces of cotton in graduated shades of charcoal. I did not stir the fabric during the dying process since I wanted it to have a mottled look which I felt would appear more realistically as shadows on the surface. After the grays were ironed and placed in a light to dark order, I numbered each piece with a piece of tape. While examining the original drawing I assigned a particular shade to each building face and noted that number on my drawing. By adding 1/2 inch to the width of each section and a bit extra in height, each shade of gray was sliced and consequently seamed into one unit which would represent the entire house. Seams were pressed in the direction of the darkest strip. This seamed section had to match with the drawing in both length and width.

In proceeding with the house, a piece of tear-away interfacing was cut as a base on which to work and chosen fabrics for the house interior and curtains were also cut. The interior fabric, a dark gray, was centered on the tear-away and the curtain fabric, a cabbage rose design with beiges, blues and browns, was placed on top. Lastly the seamed gray section was added. Now the paper drawing was carefully positioned so that the vertical seams lined up with those on the drawing. After pinning, I sewed around all the windows and proceeded to finish them as outlined in the chapter on construction.

"Crazy Quilt Victorian at 1005"
(1993) - 58" x 48"
author

With the drawing as a guide, sections of the roof were cut from freezer paper and used as a template for pressing the raw edges of roof fabric over. Before the roof was attached to the house, two pieces of narrow cording were inserted between the house and the lower roof line. One piece of the purchased cording was white and the other had black and white stripes. Their raw edges were tucked into seams or slipped under the roof. A chimney template was cut from freezer paper and edges were pressed under.

The porch was completed as a separate unit. The basic lines of the porch were drawn on a piece of Solvy (water soluble stabilizer) and a piece of black netting was pinned on to it. A combination of laces and braids were sewed to the netting while it was secured in a hoop. The spindles on the porch were formed with a decorative machine stitch. After the structure was complete, it was submerged in water so that the Solvy would dissolve. After trimming the excess netting the porch could now be sewn to the house. A Victorian lady cut from fabric which had Wonder-Under on the back was slipped under the porch before it was secured.

Creating a "Crazy Quilt" scene can be a real challenge; first in gathering every conceivable landscape oriented fabric you have hoarded over the years and, secondly, in deciding which to discard. I began with the sky and actually cut irregular shapes out of about fifteen pale prints. After lots of pinning and scrutinizing, I sewed the pieces to a half yard of muslin. Decorative stitches outlining each fabric shape completed the sky. Next a few asymmetrical shapes were cut from a variety of greens and manipulated on the design wall. The right, left, and foreground areas were sewn on separate sections of muslin and decorative stitches were added. Once each unit was nearly complete the four sections were seamed together and overlapping areas were finished.

None of the garden fabrics that I was working with seemed to be "quite right" for the prominent area in front of the porch. I really wanted ferns and flowers that more closely resembled a Victorian garden. With green netting as a base and Solvy (dissolving interfacing) underneath, I placed the two layers in a spring tension hoop and made my own ferns using free motion sewing machine techniques. Decorative stitches from the Pfaff and a variety of threads made fast work of the flowers. The lace doily underlying the garden was an afterthought. Every Crazy Quilt needs a bit of lace and I did remember that I have more that a "bit" in my stash.

Now it was time to attach the house. The interfacing first had to be removed and then the house was pinned to the Crazy Quilt background. To give the illusion of the mansion emerging from its surroundings, portions of the background patches were extended over the edges of the house. The house itself was hand-sewn to its background scene while the overlapping patches were finished by machine.

Quilting would now be the focus. The entire landscape was centered on a thin cotton batting with the backing fabric underneath. Both the backing and batting were at least ten inches larger than the designed landscape as border strips would be added later. After pin basting, the design was quilted with transparent nylon thread using free machine techniques. Each irregular shape of both sky and background were traced while sections of the house were also outlined.

Once quilted, the borders now needed to be added. With a plastic square and a yard stick straight lines were drawn along the perimeter of the fabric picture. Border strips were then sliced, seamed together and sewn to the quilt. Corners were carefully mitered and hand sewn. After quilting the border the addition of a sleeve for hanging and binding completed the frame. Lastly a fabric name plaque was added.

A close-up of 1005 with its machine embroidered garden.

WHITE'S CASTLE
1850's - 1913

FOURTH AND MAYNARD STREET
WILLIAMSPORT, PA

Although West Fourth Street was still a dusty lane lined with small frame houses and scattered farms in the late 1860's, growth in both population and wealth were becoming evident. In the ten years between 1860 and 1870 over 11,000 people had settled in Williamsport. Many of these newcomers were highly educated and excited about this new frontier in the wilderness.

As chief engineer for the construction of a canal system, Robert Faries designed and directed the building of a vast network of waterways that connected many of the small towns that were now springing up on the banks of the Susquehanna. Along with travel and communication improvements came other modern conveniences. In 1857 the Williamsport Gas Company began supplying energy to its few customers. As a charter member of the gas company, Faries fought for years against all those who felt that gas was too dangerous to be used.

It is not known when Robert Faries began construction on his own house; however it is evident that he intended to incorporate as much of his past engineering knowledge as he could. His castle, as it was called, included elements of Italiante, Moorish, and Gothic architecture. Located on an elevated mound near the rear of a 2 1/2 acre lot, the house was built of brick which was then stuccoed and marked to resemble stone. Colossal towers flanked by stone archways and walled porches, would have been a comforting sight to any knight returning from the Crusades.

After Faries' death the house was bought by John White, a lumberman, and became known as White's Castle. For forty years the White's lived on West Fourth Street and witnessed the changes brought about by the wealth of their neighbors.

In 1913 it was announced that White's Castle was at last for sale. A prospective buyer had been found and she had announced her intention to use the huge mansion as a rooming house.

At this same time J. Roman Way, who lived directly across the street, was completing extensive renovations to modernize his home, built in the early 1850's by Judge Maynard. The turret had been removed, the roof line changed, and dormers were added. When Way found out that a boarding house was to be established across the street he was enraged! The value of his house and the neighborhood would be in jeopardy.

Without hesitation Roman Way purchased White's Castle and proceeded to have it demolished. The task was a formidable undertaking as it took many hammer blows to weaken the mortar and five layers of brick underlying it.

Once the task was complete, Way fulfilled his lifetime dream of building a beautiful garden which he could view through his front windows. Eventually his park was presented to the city. In the original bequest it is stated that money may never exchange hands within the park boundaries. To this day Way's wishes are upheld. When craft and art shows are annually held in the park, vendors are asked to walk outside the iron fence to execute any transactions of currency.

In 1941 Roman Way's house opened its doors as the Lycoming Historical Museum. After 21 years fire destroyed the building and much of its contents. By 1967 it was torn down entirely, making way for the construction of the present museum which still occupies the spot from which one can admire Roman Way's beautiful garden and envision the castle which once rose from its center.

Top:
An early photo of White's Castle.

Middle Left:
Judge Maynard's house that was purchased
by Roman Way.

Middle Right:
The Maynard house after being raised three feet
and "modernized" by Roman Way.

Bottom:
The entrance to Way's Garden - 1993.

POPULATION OF
WILLIAMSPORT
1808 - 280
1810 - 365
1820 - 660
1830 - 1140
1840 - 1535
1850 - 1615
1860 - 5664
1870 - 16030
1880 - 18934
1886 - 28000

1990 - 31993

"IT SHALL BE CALLED WAY'S GARDEN"

This book would not have been complete without a quilt of White's Castle. Not only is the structure itself intriguing, but it appears completely out-of-place here in the heart of Pennsylvania. Unlike most of the early mansions that were lost to fire its demise came at the hand of a neighbor, Roman Way. He was truly a man of action; a character to be reckoned with.

In designing this quilt, I examined all the windows in Roman Way's house and decided to concentrate on the shape of the third floor turret window even though Way eventually decided to remove that section of his own house. The tall, narrow Gothic shape was both pleasing to look at and had fewer crossbars to deal with.

After drawing a frontal view of White's Castle and selecting the appropriate fabrics, I proceeded to construct the house in much the same manner as outlined in the chapter on construction. The lower front section, however, was treated as a faced applique. With lining fabric placed over the right side of the stone fabric, the arch shapes were stitched, trimmed, and turned. The central tower was treated as an applique with its raw edges ironed under, and stitched into place.

Only after the house was complete could the size of the window frame be determined. Since the castle was being viewed from a distance the window had to be quite large. Using very rough measurements, the background consisting of ground, mountain, and painted sky fabric was pieced together. After placing the castle on its mound, lines to indicate the borders of the window were drawn with chalk. Narrow strips of lighter fabric were first seamed on the lines, and then the entire window frame was appliqued to the plaster-like beige that represented the interior walls of the turret. After quilting, the beige, strip-pieced section, was added above the window to give the illusion of a decorative molding. The bare black tree, applied primarily as an iron-on applique, was stitched to the foreground at the suggestion of a friend.

The entire quilt is quite simplistic with few, but very special fabrics. Almost any Attic Window quilt design can be used to add dimension and drama to a simple landscape.

*"It Shall Be Called
Way's Garden"
(1994) - 50" x 80"
author*

A NIGHT OF HORROR JUNE 11, 1889

THE ANTES CREEK FLOOD

(EDITOR'S NOTE: The following is excerpted from a personal account in the June 11, 1889, Gazette and Bulletin by George W. Youngman Jr. about the loss of his family and his brother William's in the flood of June 1. The two families lived in adjacent houses along the west bank of the Antes Creek about two miles south of Antes Fort, where they operated a woolen mill. The Youngman property is still owned by descendants.)

BEFORE THE FLOOD

We had a little commencement of our home school on Friday, and the following visitors were present: Mrs. John F. Carothers, Mrs. J. F. Hull and daughter, and Miss Maggie Pfouts of Jersey Shore... Mrs. Hull and Mrs. Carothers left early in the evening. I took them to the station in a wagon and they took the train for Newberry.

On my return we took tea at the usual hour. Mrs. Youngman entertained them with music until between 9 and 10 o'clock. It was constantly raining, and I had fears of the dam (upstream on the creek) breaking. We retired at 11 o'clock, but couldn't sleep on account of the violent rain and wind. But having lived along the creek, and being well acquainted with the highest water and knowing the danger lines... my brother Will and I rested easily on knowledge of these facts and considered our houses safe...

EARLY SATURDAY MORNING

At 2 A.M.. Saturday my wife and I arose, being unable to sleep on account of the violence of the storm. I procured a lantern and an umbrella and went to the creek. The rest of the family and guests were still in bed.

I called to my brother Will and told him there was danger of the dam breaking. In a few minutes he came out of his house with a lantern. We stood at the main bridge near our houses, the creek being bank full, having our hands on the railing and fearing to pass over to arouse Mr. Harmon, who lived on the opposite side. Without warning the bridge suddenly gave way with a crash, and was instantly swept below. We then proceeded up the creek to the next foot bridge opposite the mill, and crossed half way over, but finding it dangerous to proceed, returned. I stopped at my house and reported the stream a dangerous condition.

During all this time the rain was pouring down in torrents and the creek was rising very rapidly. When it approached the danger line, we were still four feet higher. We sat upon the porch with our lanterns in hand watching the rising angry waters. When they reached the danger line and approached the lower story, my brother went towards his house and said the dam had broken. I then proceeded up the creek to the next foot bridge and crossed half way over, but finding it dangerous to proceed further, returned and woke up Mr. Marcus and family, and also the family of Mr. Bastian...

My brother then called out that he thought the dam had broken, and I replied that I thought so, too...

SCENE IN THE HOUSE

I immediately entered the house and found all the family and guests up and dressed. I told them I thought the dam had broken and that the water would recede in five minutes.

While I was conversing with them and assuring them that there was no immediate danger, I passed through the sitting room and kitchen to look to the safety of the barn and the horses and found eight to ten feet of water passing between the house and the barn with the swiftness of an avalanche. This showed me for the first time that we were cut off from retreat to the mountain.

I had all the family retire to the school room

in the house. The water now began to dash against the house, and floating trees, logs and other rubbish began to break in the south end of the building.

As the water rushed through the house, and as it was struck by floating timbers, it would tremble and cause consternation among the twelve inmates. I endeavored to calm their fears by telling them that the dam had broken and that I momentarily expected the water to begin to fall.

But instead of receding it increased in volume and the floating trees and timber came in greater quantity and force than ever.

While they were confined in this room, I heard the kitchen and room overhead cut loose from the main building and float away. I said nothing to alarm them but in two minutes the porch broke loose and floated off, and in less than five minutes more, the parlor, hall, and room overhead cut loose from the main building and disappeared in the madly rushing waters.

This left a building in which we were imprisoned only 16 by 32 feet in size, with two rooms. Finally the room south of the one in which the family and guests were collected broke away, leaving them in a sixteen-foot room on the north.

Before this I had become convinced that we must all be lost, and I notified my family and guests that they must prepare to save their lives. I said to the women "Doff your superfluous clothing," which they quickly did...

AN IMPRESSIVE SCENE

Miss Phelps, the governess, heroically endeavored to calm their fears by declaring that the house and family should not be destroyed. They carried with them into the room a large family Bible from the flooded room below. She turned to the 2nd verse of the 43rd chapter of Isaiah and read it aloud...

The room in which we were gave a lurch to the southward and leaned at an angle of almost forty-five degrees. Miss Phelps then went among the frightened friends and with her hands upraised and her face beaming as it appeared to me, with the radiance of the face of Joan of Arc, and declaring that she knew that this family would and should be certainly saved.

I drew her to the window and pointed to the rushing torrent beneath and said, "Miss Phelps, you have a great deal of faith, but when we drop into that seething cauldron we cannot live a minute."

THE PARTING SCENE

She then reiterated the same declaration with great emphasis and solemnity. By this time all were cognizant of their certain death.

My daughter Mary came to me and placing her arms about my neck, kissed me and said, "Papa, we will all go to Heaven together." My wife, with her babe in her arms, approached and kissed me and said, "Are you ready?" I replied, "I am." Then she said, "I am glad."

Miss Phelps then said, pointing to my wife, "I know what you are," and she replied, "I know what you are." I replied, "I know what the whole of you are!"

The danger had now become more threatening, with the flood still increasing in volume. Miss Phelps now took the keys for her trunk from her pocket, opened it, and seizing her jewels, placed them on her fingers and body, remarking to the rest that this was the hour to wear jewelry.

IN THE JAWS OF DEATH

Satisfied of our fate I tore my necktie off, threw off my gum boots, rolled down my collar and rolled up my sleeves. My wife looked at me with anguish depicted on her countenance and frantically asked me what I was doing. I informed her that I was going to be prepared to save their lives and my own, if possible. My little boy Reynolds did the same.

Two minutes after Miss Phelps had placed her jewelry on her person and we had made preparation to battle with death, the east side of the room fell into the fierce torrent with a crash, and the twelve inmates were engulfed.

I kept watching for some of them to appear. The wreck proceeded in the torrent in the direction of the creamery some 500 feet below. Here I found Miss Phelps and hauled her on the wreck in a drowning condition.

I brushed the mud from her face and she gasped: "George, what will we do?" I replied that, "I told you before our only hope of life was to catch on to some secure tree or leap from the wreck when it struck the banks."

We were not two minutes in going half a mile when we struck a sharp curve in the creek among the wreck of houses, which were rapidly moving. Just before this two long timbers struck the wreck ahead and it ran under the timbers.

The current struck the timbers and one struck me, which I pushed aside. The other sheered from the wreck, taking Miss Phelps and Reynolds with it.

Seizing my niece Emily Hull, I dragged her on the drift dislocating her arm in the effort. She and I were now isolated on this drift until eleven o'clock Saturday morning, not knowing that my brother Will's house had gone until I found his boy Walter (dead) in the wreck with me.

In the scramble for life, my son Reynolds exclaimed, "Don't hold me - save the rest - I can swim!"

To prevent the little girl, Emily, from perishing I laid her in some hay and lifted her into a tree, where she remained for an hour until the flood subsided and she was rescued. I had to lie by her side to keep her warm.

Thinking over the loss of life while lying there, I began to count them on my fingers, and as I enumerated the names of the lost each time I'd miss little Charlie (his 3 year-old son), and she would call from under the hay each time, "You have missed little Charlie."

THE LOST AND SAVED

Of the twelve in the wrecked house, the following were drowned:

> Mrs. Tillie Youngman, 38
> and infant, 6 weeks
> Anna Mary Youngman, 17
> Ralph Youngman, 9
> Phoebe Youngman, 6
> Charles Youngman, 3
> Miss Eliza Phelps, 24
> Miss Aggie Pfouts, 38

The saved were:

> George W. Youngman, Jr.
> Reynolds Youngman, 13
> Gardner Youngman, 10
> Emily Hull (niece), 11

"I have lost everything," said Mr. Youngman, "even the clothes I have on had to be furnished me. I cannot go back to that dreadful place again!"

William Youngman, his brother, was found in an insensible condition in the wreck. His house was destroyed and his wife, Margaret, 35, and two children, Walter, 9, and Emily, 4, were drowned.

On the opposite side of the creek the house of J. M. Harmon was wrecked and one boy, Ray, aged 5, drowned.

After this terrible avalanche of water it was learned that the dam did not break - that it did not contribute to swelling the waters any more rapidly than the natural cause. Only part of a dirt embankment gave way. It is Mr. Youngman's opinion that the surface water, which accumulated rapidly from the tremendous downpour, rushed through the gorge in the mountain from Nippenose Valley because it was the only outlet, and bore death and desolation in its course. The theory is undoubtedly the correct one, and the terrible loss of life at the woolen mills will be a sad reminder for generations of the great calamity.

THE LAST CHAPTER

A concluding chapter was written to this saga in 1989, when the family Bible was returned to the great grandson of George W. Youngman by the heirs of the lad who helped recover the body of Elizabeth Phelps that June in 1889. Oral family history recounts that the governess was found ensnared high up in a tree by the long strands of her hair, and that Bible clutched in her arms was still open to Isaiah.

Isaiah chapter 43 verse 2: "When thou passest through the waters, I will be with thee; and through the rivers, they shall not overflow thee."

This Bible is now on permanent display at the Lycoming County Historical Museum.

Although the Youngman descendants still enjoy summer residences located along Antes Creek, the stone mill is the only original remaining structure that survived the flood. A century of changing ownership and disuse had turned the stone mill into an eyesore and a subject of safety concern to its neighbors. Extensive renovations have just been completed and "The Paint Mill", as it is now called, has become available for private gathering and receptions. Its name signifies its wartime use as a factory where limestone was ground into "battleship gray" pigment for paint production.

FAMILY PORTRAIT *includes many of those swept away by raging Antes Creek 100 years ago. Hattie Leinbach, a friend spared the tragedy, in in back at left. Mary Youngman, in back at center, drowned at 17. Reynolds Youngman, in back at right, survived, as did Gardner Youngman, middle left. Elizabeth Phelps, governess, holds toddler Charles Youngman. He was three when he drowned and she was 24. The girl to her right, Phoebe Youngman, 6, and the seated boys, cousins Ralph and Walter Youngman, both 9, all perished. Also drowned, but not in photo, were: Tillie Youngman, 38; Phelps, six weeks; Maggie Pfouts, 38; Margaret Youngman, 35, and Emily, 4. In addition, a neighbor across the creek, Ray Harmon, 5, drowned.*

"THE MILL ON ANTES CREEK"

Antes Creek, a limestone stream located a short distance south west of Williamsport, rises from the Enchanted Spring and runs four miles through the Gap to empty into the Susquehanna River.

Designed and executed by Judith Youngman, this quilt depicts the woolen mill that was owned and operated by her husband's ancestors over one hundred years ago. From the steep slopes behind their house, they would have been able to view the mill as she has chosen to portray it.

It was over ten years ago that I first read the newspaper account of the flood of 1889. At that time I was so moved by the story that I cut it out and placed it in a file. Years later on a trip to a quilt conference, Judith and I found ourselves talking about the rich local history that surrounded our area. One thought led to another and by the time we arrived at Quilting-By-The-Lake a new mission had been born. I would search for fascinating stories that revolved around old Williamsport houses and construct the quilts, and she would concentrate on the mill.

The arrival of a bolt of an unusual Hoffman Bail print summoned Judith to begin her quilt. At last the perfect "stone" fabric for the mill had been found. As a rough outline was prepared the scene began to take on the aura of a piece of folk art. Appropriate fabrics were selected to complete the landscape and add to its primitive character. Traditional applique techniques were followed in the construction and both machine and hand quilting added just the right amount of texture.

Antes Creek

The Paint Mill - 1993

"The Mill on Antes Creek"
(1994) - 42" x 34"
Judith Youngman

Close-up of White's Castle on page 41

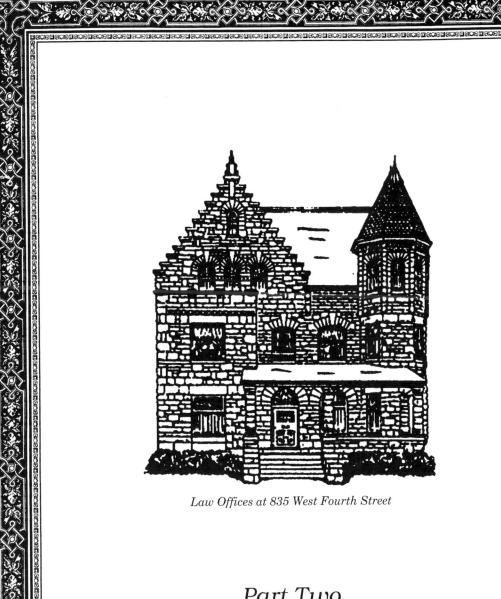

Law Offices at 835 West Fourth Street

Part Two
BUILDING
A FABRIC HOUSE

Gathering Materials

1. A PHOTO of the house - A front view is the easiest to work with.

2. DRAWING SUPPLIES - graph paper ruled 1/4" or 1/8 " (12" x 18" or larger), pencil, eraser, rulers.

3. FABRIC - 100% cottons - Each piece must be large enough to cover the area it is used to represent..

a. INTERIOR of the house - Pale yellows or golds indicate light within the house while dark shades portray an unlit house. This fabric should have very little texture.

b. CURTAIN fabric - Light prints with very tiny delicate designs create a lacy effect.

c. EXTERIOR house fabric - Red or rust calico becomes brick; slate blues or tans represent stone; delicate stripes are perfect for siding. There are fabrics available today that closely resemble brick, stone, stucco, or wood surfaces. Buy these hard to find geometric designs when you see them.

d. ROOFING fabric - A dark colored fabric seems to work best, even if the actual house you are duplicating has new white shingles. With a dark roof, the house appears to have a frame and all its features are accented.

e. TRIM fabrics - Narrow striped fabrics or wallpaper-type border prints are perfect for shutters, porch steps, and any feature that would benefit from their use.

4. LACES, BRAIDS and CORDING - Lace can be used to represent the gingerbread type trims that outline roof edges on Victorian houses as well as porch railings and other decorative features. Narrow braids are perfect for dividing windows and decorative cording can be slipped under the edge of a roof.

5. INTERFACING - Nonwoven, medium weight interfacing (tear-away is best if you can get it) will provide a foundation for all our sewing and should be approximately 2" to 3" larger than the house drawing.

6. CARDBOARD - Thin cardboard (i.e. cereal box) will be used for making roof and door templates.

7. SPRAY STARCH or SIZING

8. THREAD - Choose colors to match your fabrics. Transparent nylon thread (made especially for quilters) is useful to have on hand.

9. SEWING MACHINE and BASIC SUPPLIES

335 Rural Avenue

Just for Fun!

With permission this article was printed from the book Modern American Dwellings - 1897 by Donald J. Berg - Antiquity Reprints

This design represents a dwelling planned and erected for his own use by W. C. McCabe of Eaton, Ohio.

Mr. McCabe gives the actual cost of the house as $3271.18, the principal items being lumber and carpenter work, $1562.52; plumbing and brick wall in basement and chimneys, $123.30; lathing and plastering, $165.16; painting and varnishing, $174.35; glass and glazing, $68.21; hardware and nails, $95.90; electric light wiring, $26.60; furnace and fittings, $193.20; grates and mantels, $112.55; tin and galvanized iron work, $68.96. The items also include wall paper, $92.60, and a safe in the china closet, the cost of which is given as $68. To this total may be added the work outside of the house, covering grading, stone steps, walks, etc., $210.80, making a grand total of $3,481.98. Mr. McCabe states that the above items were carefully kept during the erection of the house and is the net cost to him, the builder's profit not being included. If this were added it would probably increase the cost about 10 percent.

Drawing Your House

All of us remember spending lots of time drawing pictures in elementary school. With crayons, we drew our families, our pets, our summer vacations, and of course, the house we lived in. If you've forgotten how wonderful these drawings were, rest assured that they were probably very similar to those drawn by any 6 year old today. Now the hysteria begins! That house we drew with the pointed roof, tiny window, giant sized door, and the lollipop tree is not quite the image we want to hang above our fireplace for all our friends to view. With some determination, guidance, and an eraser, I'm certain you can draw a house that everyone will recognize and admire. A very simple outline drawing, without elaborate embellishment, is all that is necessary.

1. Begin by closely examining a photo of the house. If you're lucky, the bushes and trees will cooperate and allow for a clear view. Hint: Winter is a good time to take photos. A frontal shot will be the easiest to examine and draw without lots of involvement with perspective. Here are some questions to answer.

   a. Is the house taller than wide or vice versa? Use a ruler if you must to determine the answer.

   b. How many stories or floors are there? The attic (roof area) may be more or less than a full story.

   c. Examine the vertical divisions and compare their size. A ruler can be used to measure these sections on your snapshot. (i.e. Left portion is 2 1/2 cm., right 4 cm.) If you can visit the actual house, you can measure the distance by pacing it off. (i.e. Left section is 8 paces, Right is 11 paces) These numbers can be converted to inches. (i.e. Each pace can represent 1" on your graph paper.)

2. Choose a piece of graph paper (ruled 1/4") that is approximately the size of the finished house. Working with a piece 12" x 18" is quite manageable as it turns easily under the sewing machine, yet has windows that allow for details. For a larger fabric house purchase larger sheets of graph paper or tape several together.

3. Place the paper in accordance with the overall shape of the exterior of the house.

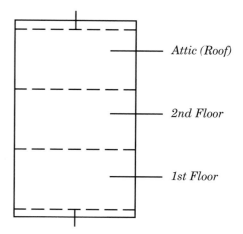

Attic (Roof)

2nd Floor

1st Floor

4. Draw a line about 1" from both the bottom and the top edge of the paper. If a tall peak extends above the roof this line must be dropped to accommodate the height.

5. Divide the remaining space between these lines into the number of floors in the structure. The paper can be manipulated by folding or measured by ruler and divided. These divisions will be used as a guide and can be marked with a small slash on the edge of the paper. (Drawn above)

6. Divide the paper in half vertically by placing a slash on the paper's top or bottom edge. This will also serve only as a guide for marking other vertical lines.

7. Draw any vertical lines which indicate where specific sections of the house forms edges (i.e. an L-shaped design, turret, etc.)

8. Carefully study the doors and windows in your photo. Several generalizations can usually be made. Windows are usually the same size, balanced, spaced evenly, and line up above each other. Both doors and windows tend to end on the same level close to the floor lines you have indicated. Consider the questions below.

   a. Are the windows wider than the door or the same?

   b. Is the distance from the door to the first window the same as the width of the door or less? What about the distances between the windows?

   c. Are the windows of the second floor directly above those on the first floor? Usually they are.

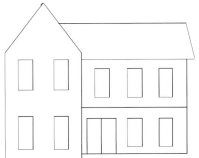

9. Draw the doors and windows on the first floor and then draw the second floor windows.

10. Draw the top and bottom horizontal roof edges. By viewing the house from ground level, the roof may appear very flat when in fact it has more height. If the roof looks too flat, give it more height.

11. Sketch the slant on only one side of the house. If it looks good, try folding along the slant to easily trace the same slant on the opposite side.

12. Make a tracing of your completed drawing. Taping the original drawing, with tracing paper on top, onto a window pane works well. One copy of your drawing will be destroyed as it is sewn over in the next construction steps.

Note: In drawing the Peck House, I used an opaque projector to focus a photo of the house onto a sheet of graph paper taped to the wall. This is a procedure that could be investigated more thoroughly using either opaque or slide projection. In my work I found that I eventually re-drew most of the sketched lines, however, since the drawing was to be quite large, it was helpful in placing and sizing windows as well as drawing roof lines.

Actual drawing of Peck House - 34" x 28"

Actual drawing of 1005 - 24" x 22"

Constructing Your House

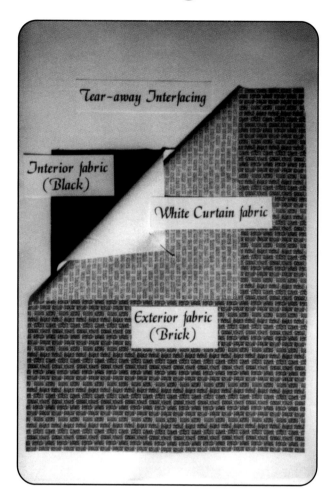

1. Choose fabrics and layer on top of tear-away interfacing.

On top of the interfacing, first lay the fabric used to represent the inside of the house (light or dark). Place the curtain fabric on top. Lastly add the fabric chosen for the outside of the house.

2. Pin drawing onto your layered fabric and interfacing.

Be certain that the curtain and interior fabric is under all the windows.

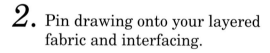

3. Stitch around the basic house outline.

With a straight machine stitch, sew through the drawing right on top of the pencil lines. Begin under the roof line and complete the entire house outline. Do not trace the top of the roof.

4. Stitch around each window and then remove the drawing.

Follow the basic window opening. Do not consider any of the ledges or moldings at this time. Carefully tear away all of the paper drawing.

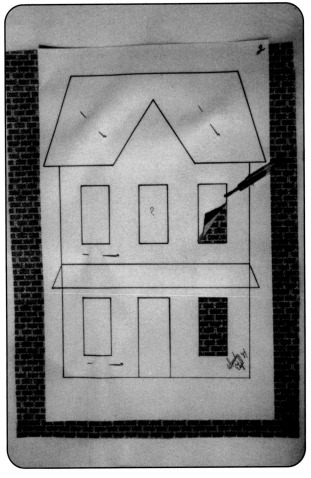

5. Cut away the exterior fabric covering the windows.

Lift the top layer of fabric with a pin, snip a small slit, and carefully cut away the fabric hiding the curtain fabric.

6. Draw the curtain shape.

On the exposed fabric, or on the interfacing on the back, draw the shape with a pencil or washout marker. A simple pattern can be drawn on one of the pieces of paper torn from the windows. Always allow a gap between the curtain lines at the top of the window. Finishing the edge and adding crossbars will be easier.

7. Sew over the curtain shape.

With a straight machine stitch, sew over the curtain line that was just drawn. Use thread to match the curtain fabric.

8. Remove the excess curtain fabric.

Carefully cut away the excess curtain fabric revealing the gold or dark interior fabric.

9. Finish the curtain edge.

Either satin stitch along the edge or use a very narrow picot trim or lace to cover both the raw edge as well as the line of machine stitching.

10. Draw and then sew the crossbars.

Decide on the number of crossbars and draw them with a pencil or washout marker using a ruler or guide ... narrow 1/4" masking tape might be useful. Finish these lines by straight stitching over very narrow ribbon or braid, or satin stitch with colored thread.

11. Finish the top ledge and sill of the windows.

Narrow trims or ribbons can be stitched over these edges or they can be satin stitched. If no shutters are to be added, the entire opening can be satin stitched.

12. Prepare the shutters.

If a narrow striped fabric is used, spray with starch and press the two vertical edges under. Using a 3x5 card, measure the height of your shutters and cut the card on that line. Use this card to iron all the shutters over, assuring a uniform height. Use the same procedure for any fabric shutters. Pin each shutter in place and sew along the outer edges with a straight stitch.

13. Construct and add the door.

Make a simple cardboard template for the door. Spray your chosen fabric with starch and iron the fabric edges over the template. Do not fold the bottom edge of the door under the template. Pin the door to the house and top stitch along the outer edge. If a window is wanted, lay a small piece of curtain fabric under the door and proceed as in step 5. Tiny door knobs can be purchased from shops featuring doll houses.

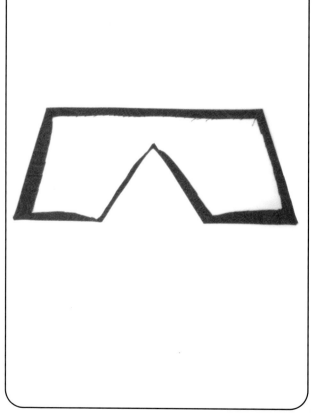

14. Prepare the roof.

Make a cardboard template using the original drawing. Place the template on the wrong side of the roof fabric and cut about 1/2" from the pattern. Spray the fabric with starch and iron the edges over the template. Note: Where a sharp peak divides the roof, iron each side separately. Several separate roof templates might be necessary.

15. Attach the roof.

Pin the ironed roof onto the house. A piece of lace can be slipped under the bottom edge and caught as the roof edge is stitched. The outer edges of the lace are left loose and are tucked under at a later step when the house is added to the background. Do not sew beyond the sides of the house. The top of the roof is not sewn down at this time allowing the excess building fabric to be removed.

16. Prepare the porch roof and attach to the house.

Make a cardboard template for the roof and iron the sprayed fabric over its edges. Pin this roof to the house and attach only along the top edge with a straight machine stitch. You should be able to lift the bottom edge to slide porch pillars and lace trim underneath later.

17. Prepare and attach the porch floor.

The porch floor consists of a slice of fabric that is longer than the width of the house. The depth of the porch is dependent upon the size and perspective view of the house. Once the measurement is determined the top and bottom edges of the strip of porch floor are sprayed and ironed under. Next the top edge of the floor is sewn to the house. This will cover the bottom raw edge of the door.

18. Add porch spindles and rails.

If individual porch spindles made from trims or lace are to be used, they must be measured and cut, pinned in place and stitched to the house. A railing made from lace can now be sewn along the top and bottom raw edges of the spindles. Often a section of lace can be used to represent both the spindles and the railing as one piece and can be top stitched in place.

19. Attach porch pillars.

Cut sections of lace or trims long enough to be slipped under the porch roof and extend below the entire porch floor. Pin these in place so that the raw edges of the porch rails are tucked under the pillars. Stitch the rails to the house. The bottom raw edge will be tucked under the porch floor when the house is attached to its background.

20. Attach the front edge of the porch roof and remove the excess brick fabric from behind the upper roof.

An additional piece of lace can be slipped under the porch before it is sewn down. Do not stitch beyond the actual sides of the house.

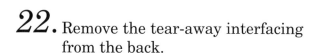

21. Prepare and attach the porch steps and the chimney.

Steps can be made from a striped fabric or by sewing small strips of light and dark fabrics into a unit. The sides and bottom edges of the unit can be ironed under while the upper edge is slipped under the porch floor. Very often the sides of the steps are softened with bushes added later. Make a cardbord chimney template and iron the sprayed fabric over it. Slip the chimney under the upper roof edge.

22. Remove the tear-away interfacing from the back.

Carefully remove the interfacing being sure not to cut into any of the sewn threads. Some areas will be very small and are better left intact. I use a seam ripper.

23. Fold the fabric along the sides of the house to the back.

Cut off any curtain or interior fabric to decrease the bulk along the fold.

24. Prepare the background.

The background can be made from just one fabric, or can be made by sewing a piece of green (grass) to a piece of blue (sky). Cut the green fabric to indicate a horizon, iron the cut edge under, pin it to the sky and top stitch on top of the green edge. More elaborate compositions can include mountain ranges. They are handled by this simple top stitching method. If transparent nylon thread is used the sewing line disappears.

25. Layer the background, batting or fleece, and backing for the quilt.

By pinning these three layers of the quilt at this point , the project will be quilted as you add the remaining elements of the scene.

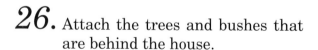

26. Attach the trees and bushes that are behind the house.

Refer to the landscape section to make greenery. All the trees and bushes shown here are faced appliques. Pin the individual plants to the background and attach them by stitching along their outer edges. I practiced free motion stitching (darning) techniques using transparent nylon thread.

27. *Attach the house.*

Pin the house to the background. Stitch along the entire outer edge. When coming to the lace trim under the roofs, cut it back and fold under the raw edge using a pin. Top stitch over these edges to secure them. Retrace other features of the house that need to be accentuated, (i.e. around the windows, doors, under roof edges, etc.)

28. Prepare and add the foreground bushes.

Refer to the section on bushes. Top stitch these bushes to your composition. Use this foliage to cover the outer raw edges of the porch floor as well as softening the edges of the steps. Add extra quilting if it is needed.

29. Frame and enjoy!

Add a fabric border if you choose and finish the outer edge with a binding. A sleeve attached to the back allows the piece to be hung properly. The house can also be mounted in a wooden frame or secured in an oval or round quilting hoop.

"Springtime on Main Street"
(1993) - 57" x 30" - Judith Youngman

SPECIAL FEATURES

In Part One of this book each of the historial quilts has a detailed description that explains just how specific features were tackled. Studying these write-ups may help you solve your architectural challenge.

Turrets & Towers

TURRETS AND TOWERS

Dormers

DORMERS

Using a slightly different fabric to represent a turret or tower helps define its shape. After ironing under the vertical sides of your fabric to the exact width of the tower, place this section on top of your layered fabrics (Step #1) and carefully position the paper pattern on top lining up the drawn lines with the tower section. From this point proceed with Step #3 in the construction section.

Dormers are prepared as separate structures on tear-away interfacing. The sides and bottom edges are ironed under and the windows are layered and sewn as outlined earlier in this section. When complete, the dormer is sewn to the roof and its peak is covered with a strip of purchased bias or fabric with its edges ironed under.

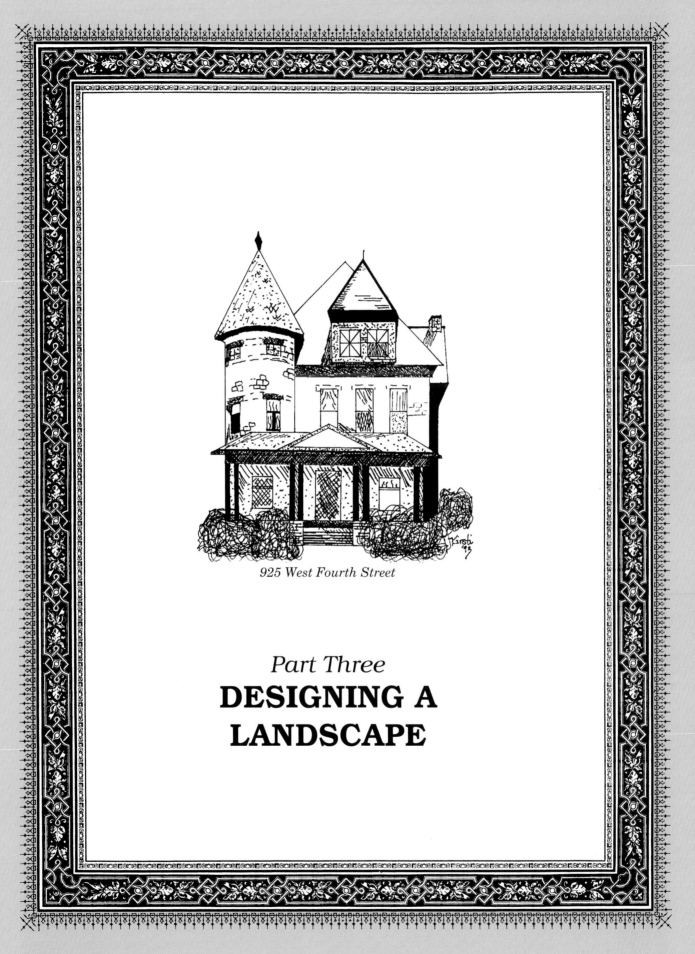

925 West Fourth Street

Part Three
DESIGNING A LANDSCAPE

Choosing A Setting

There are numerous possibilities for a setting in which to place your house. Below are several suggestions which might spark your imagination.

1. A SIMPLE or CAMEO-LIKE SETTING consisting of a single fabric (soft beige, light blue, etc.) may be all that is desired. If this is the direction you choose to take, I usually add a few appliqued bushes along the house's foundation and perhaps a tree or bush, partially hidden behind the house to soften all the straight lines.

2. An ACTUAL or FICTIONAL LANDSCAPE depicting all the elements of a complete scene might be a challenge worth attempting. (Ex. "An Afternoon At The Peter Herdic House", "Victorian Winter in 1872", "Castle By the Sea")

3. A TRADITIONAL QUILT BLOCK setting may be appropriate if several houses need to be highlighted. (i.e. house sampler with sashing strips, attic window design, etc.), (Ex. "Log Homes of the North", "Lycoming Log Homes", and "Victorian Homes")

4. The completed house may become a part of a PIECED SCENE which consists of traditional pieced trees or even a "Crazy Quilt" design. (Ex. "Crazy Quilt Mansion at 1005")

5. A GARMENT or TOTE bag allows your house to travel with you. Be sure the base fabric is sturdy enough to support the many layers of fabric that make up the house. (i.e. twill, denim, etc.)

"Pat's Challenge"
(1993) - 40" x 45"
Jeanne Taylor

Growing Some Plants

After delving into the realm of landscape design you will find the desire to collect a wide variety of green fabrics. Yellow-greens, olives, grey-greens, and emerald greens are only a few of the shades found in nature. Designs and textures add variety to the list as greens with pink flowers become spring bushes and green with red dots become berry bushes. Since only small amounts are usually needed, buy as many pieces as you can afford and dare store. A wide variety of shades, values, and textures will create a realistic feeling of depth as the assortment of bushes and flowers step forward or retreat as the admirer glances upon the scene.

BUSHES AND SHRUBS

Simple Faced Applique

1. Draw a bush shape onto a small piece of non-fusible light weight interfacing.

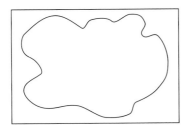

2. Place the drawing on top of the right side of the bush fabric and pin.

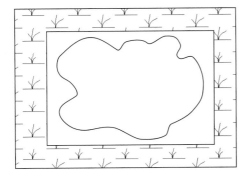

3. Sew completely around the bush on top of the drawn pencil line.

4. Trim away the excess fabric along the outside edge to approximately 1/8".

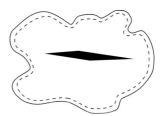

5. Cut a slit in the interfacing and pull the bush fabric through the hole turning the piece inside out. Use some smooth tool to make sure all the edges are turned to the seam line. (Crochet hook, pen with retractable point, etc.)

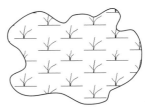

6. Carefully iron the edges so that the interfacing is hidden under the seam.

7. Attach to the background by using hand applique techniques or machine. A narrow zigzag or pin stitch using transparent nylon thread works well. Be sure the interfacing is tucked under and not showing.

NOTE: For very small appliques, the interfacing may be too bulky or tear too easily. Thin organdy works well or the bush can even be faced with another green cotton.

FREE-MOTION EMBROIDERED BUSHES AND TREES

Examples can be seen in "Victorian Winter", "Crazy Quilt Mansion", "The Mill on Antes Creek", and "Off to the Ball".

1. Materials: SOLVY (Water Soluble Stabilizer by Sulky of America), fine bridal netting called bridal illusion (cream, white, green, black), 7" spring tension embroidery hoop.

2. Layer a piece of Solvy with bridal netting on top and place into the hoop as on page 76 - step 3. (If you wish, you can draw onto the Solvy with a thin permanent pen as I did when sewing the fence below).

3. Follow instructions for darning, drop the feed dogs, and place the proper foot on the machine.

4. With the hoop under the foot, lower the needle through the netting and bring the bobbin thread up to the top while raising the needle.

Both the trees and the iron fence were sewn on netting and added to the background.

5. While holding both the top and the bobbin threads, take a few stitches to secure the thread. Cut the thread tails.

6. Draw the branches of the bush with your thread moving the hoop as you draw. Always retrace the stem as you move to another branch.

7. When complete, clip the threads and remove the netting from the hoop. Place the netting in water to dissolve the Solvy. Trim away the excess netting.

8. When attaching the bush, I prefer to turn the edge of the netting under so it is not as likely to get caught in anything while it is worked upon.

NOTE: Pieces of fabric, colored or white lace, (I used white lace in the Victorian Winter quilt), or threads can be sandwiched between the Solvy and netting to create a new dimension. In addition many new sewing machines have decorative stitches that can be used with the Solvy, netting and hoop and resemble hand embroidered designs.

A. In this photo a plant is drawn with thread using free motion darning techniques. The finished palm can be seen on page 29.

B. Here a tree cut from brown fabric and rocks from "stone" fabric are sandwiched between Solvy (on bottom) and netting (on top). The raw edges can be coated with Fray-Check but this is not necessary.

C. With brown thread the trunk is covered with stitching and the main branches are extended into the very fine fingers seen on the opposite page.

3-DIMENSIONAL BUSHES WITH ELASTIC THREAD

These bushes can be seen in the front of the Herdic House in the close-up on page 6.

1. Wind elastic thread onto a bobbin by hand, (approximately 30 - 40 turns for a bush).

2. Insert the bobbin - do not change tensions. Use regular thread on top. Match the color with the bush fabric.

3. Position fabric in a spring embroidery hoop (7" or larger). Lay the outer plastic hoop on a flat surface and place the "bush" fabric over it. Place the inner spring on top of the fabric and snap it into the hoop by squeezing it. The fabric will now touch the throat plate while you sew. (This position is the reverse of that used in embroidery.)

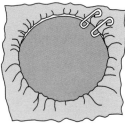

4. Slide the hoop under the needle, lower the needle through the fabric and bring it back up until the end of the elastic thread comes to the top. You will have to give it a tug to pull it through.

5. Follow machine instructions for darning: change to a darning foot, drop the feed dogs, and lower the tension bar.

6. Holding both top thread and elastic bobbin thread, secure both with a few stitches.

7. Guide the hoop with both hands as you begin sewing in the center with a grape size circle. Continue to add petal-like half circles as you move outwardly. The elastic thread will resist perfectly smooth sewing but after a bit of practice your stitches will improve. Continue until the hoop is filled.

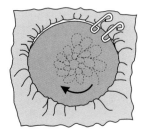

8. Remove the fabric from the hoop, (it will shrink to about half its size), trim the excess fabric to about 1/4" from the stitching, turn under and applique.

Note: If the fabric shrinks too much an extra layer of muslin or very thin batting can be layered beneath the bush fabric. Much of this depends upon the elasticity of the thread you are using.

Thanks! I was introduced to this technique in a class taught by Lois Smith of Rockville, Maryland, at a Quilting-By-The-Lake workshop.

LACE TREES & WILLOWS

A lace willow tree can be seen on page 80.

1. Draw and then construct the trunk of the tree as a faced-applique. The upper section of the trunk can be left open.

2. Make the branches by cutting strips of bias that are approximately 3/4" to 1" wide. I do not use a ruler, but instead cut freely with either a scissors or rotary cutter. Tree branches should not look like pieces of purchased bias. Spray these strips with starch and iron the edges under (humps and bumps are good).

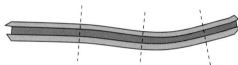

3. Slice these longer pieces into smaller sections approximately 1-1/2" to 2" long. Reserve some for longer cuts if they are needed.

4. The leaves or blossoms will be represented with clusters of lace cut from yardage. (Check bridal department of fabric store). Shades of pink and whites for spring blossoms, greens for willows and summer trees, and blacks for trees seen at dusk. Cut the lace into irregular shapes. The size depends upon your tree dimensions. If possible use several shades of the same color to add depth. In the willow tree pictured above, I dyed an old white lace dress so that I had four shades of green.

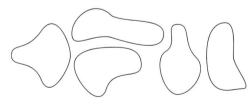

5. At this point you can work directly on your landscape, or as I did in the willow tree, on a separate piece of sky fabric that was the same as that in the landscape.

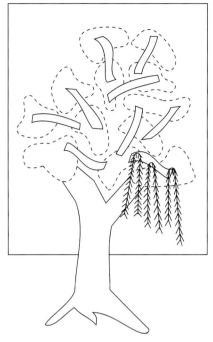

6. Position your trunk and branches and begin shaping the pieces of lace over the raw edges of the branches. With a steam iron the bias branches can be shaped to more closely resemble the tree you are designing.

7. Once you are satisfied, pin or baste all the loose pieces of your tree.

8. Secure all the loose pieces by stitching over everything with transparent nylon thread. Free motion techniques would be the easiest. In the case of my willow tree, I then used lime green thread and a decorative stitch to create the long branches of the tree. In adding these I made sure that all the sections of lace and branches were secure.

9. If you have chosen to work on a separate section of sky fabric, you will now trim the excess sky allowing approximately 1/4" for turning under. The tree is now positioned and appliqued to the landscape. In the quilting stage I sewed additional willow branches over the appliqued edge to conceal it.

Landscaping Begins

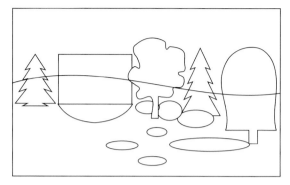

SEARCHING FOR INSPIRATION

1. A photograph of the house and surrounding you wish to construct, or photos of scenes that are of interest to you are perfect. Begin taking a camera with you to capture just such settings.

2. Paintings or prints, often depicting scenes from the time the house was constructed, are wonderful to examine. If a painter found a setting to have merit, we can benefit by examining his placement of subjects, shadings, perspective, etc. Visit frame shops where catalogs of prints are available and go to the local library and leaf through art books.

3. Scenic calendars, magazine advertisements, and travel folders often capture a mood that can be studied and interpreted. Begin a file for all those beautiful pictures that may serve as inspirations at a later date.

FORMULATING A BLUEPRINT

1. Sketch a very rough drawing of the scene you wish to complete with squares for houses and lollipop trees. Preparing a rough sketch tends to focus ideas although it is not always necessary. Very often I have an image in my head that never seems to look very interesting on paper. In those cases I simply dive into the project and begin working with the fabric elements of the scene and build my landscape one bush at a time.

2. Determine the appropriate size for the finished quilt. The size of the house will serve as a beginning. Most trees are taller than houses and if many trees are to be added, the quilt must be large enough to accommodate them. Always add some extra inches as they can easily be cut away once the scene is complete.

"Castle Rock"
(1993) - 33" x 33"
Mary Lou Doebler

CONSTRUCTING A SETTING

1. By joining a piece of sky fabric to a piece of foreground fabric (grass, ground, etc.), a design surface is available for all the separate elements that will be placed, shifted, examined, and lastly sewn to the quilt. A single piece of special fabric can also be used when creating a cameo-like setting.

2. Sky fabric can be light blue, navy, or specially designed in sunset colors. Whatever is chosen, it must not distract from the main focus of the scene. Purchased fabrics, as well as those that are hand-dyed or hand-painted, should be purchased whenever they are available.

3. There are many grass-like cottons available in fabric shops. If a green calico is to be used, it should not contain a bold texture that will distract from the house or other shrubbery. You may wish to delve into the area of fabric dying and painting to get just what you want.

4. Once the sky and foreground fabric is chosen, they can be seamed together. After cutting a gently rolling horizon, the cut edge is ironed under, pinned to the sky fabric and top stitched. After all the elements of the landscape are in place, very little of this horizon is visible. If mountains are to be a part of the landscape, they can be cut freely, edges ironed under, overlapped, and top stitched to the sky before the foreground is added. Sewing with matching or transparent thread will minimize the sewn line.

5. The front, batting, and backing of the quilt can be sandwiched at this time and basted in a few spots using safety pins. Next, this background design

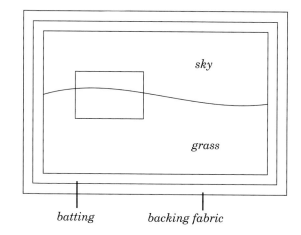

sky

grass

batting   *backing fabric*

surface needs to be pinned to a wall where it can be examined as elements are added.

6. The house that is now complete can be positioned and pinned to the background.

"I'll Paint Mine Red"
(1993)
Louise Shaffer

LET THE PLANTING BEGIN!

1. All the trees, bushes, and flower gardens must be sewn individually. (Refer to chapter on Plants) It is possible to lay tracing or tissue paper over the background fabric to make rough sketches of trees and bushes. This is especially helpful in determining the height of trees.

2. Once the placement of a cluster of bushes has been finalized, they can be carefully pinned and attached to each other where they overlap. This can be done on the machine although there is less chance of shifting if they are placed on a small flat surface (cardboard or cutting board) and stitched by hand. This cluster can now be returned to the quilt.

3. Trees are constructed individually and can be moved about until you are satisfied with their placement. The house will have to be lifted partially if trees are to be placed behind it.

Background fabric

Batting —| |— Backing

4. Once the scene appears to be complete, individual trees and bushes need to be pinned more carefully so they will not drop off as the quilt is now taken to the sewing machine.

Close-up of Herdic House Quilt on page 19

Time To Quilt

1. First the house needs to be attached by sewing along its outer edges as well as outlining its features. Be sure the house is straight and has not shifted.

2. Begin by stitching up one side, under the roof edge, and back down the opposite side. A straight machine stitch with thread to match the house or a pin stitch with either matching or nylon thread may be used. If you decide to attach the house along the edges by hand, you will probably only want to catch the background fabric. Complete the attachment and quilting of the house by straight stitching around the windows, the door, sections of the house, rooftop, chimney, and other features that would benefit from this sewing.

3. Working outward from the house, attach the bushes and trees using matching or transparent thread and a narrow zig-zag or pin stitch. Using free motion techniques with the feed dogs engaged eliminates the need to turn the entire quilt as the bushes are traced. On a very large quilt, hand appliqueing the trees and clusters of bushes may be more manageable. If this is the case they must be quilted later.

4. Quilting the sky and those areas that are void of greenery, will have to be tackled next. The sky can be filled in with either hand or machine stitches. Cloud shapes, currents of smoke, or soft, wind-like lines are perfect. An evening sky can be tied using a decorative machine stitch or even tiny crystals. A foreground section can be filled in with gentle curved lines indicating uneven ground lines or the entire area can be stippled as it was in the Herdic House Quilt (pg. 19)

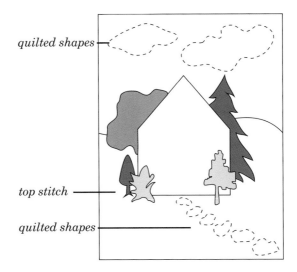

quilted shapes

top stitch

quilted shapes

If you intend to use such heavy quilting, the entire foreground should be prequilted before any of the trees, bushes, etc. are attached.

5. After the quilting is complete, the outer edges must be ruled so that borders will be straight and parallel with the outer corners of the house itself. This can be done with an assortment of quilting rulers, a yardstick, and a colored or chalk pencil. Likewise the upper edge of the quilt must be parallel with the roof lines if a front facing house is present.

6. Once borders are added and quilted, the quilt can be bound.

7. A sleeve sewn onto the back allows the quilt to be supported and hung properly. For large quilts I use aluminum clothes line props that are cut to the proper length and capped on the ends.

Option: Your quilted house can be framed professionally or placed in either an oval (17"x27") or round (23") quilting hoop. If this is the route that you have chosen to take be sure to allow extra fabric along the outer edges.

Invite Some Friends

Including figures in a house quilt is as natural as adding the trees and bushes which we all consider imperative. Although it is far easier to sketch a bush, don't let your artistic shortcomings keep you from breathing real life into your quilt!

First begin by collecting greeting cards, photos, and coloring books that feature people you feel might be appropriate. Books of paper dolls are perfect. I particularly like scenes where ladies have long dresses (no skinny legs to contend with), and big hats (little face or hair to represent).

By placing tracing paper over the figure a simple pencil sketch of the outline is made. Next this can be enlarged or decreased on a photocopy machine until the proper size is attained.

Figures that are medium in size (5" to 7") can be completed as a faced applique. With tiny people (3"-4") it is easier to trace shapes onto Wonder-Under and iron them onto the chosen fabric.

ENCIE

*See pattern section
for
additional people.*

LET'S BEGIN

FACED APPLIQUE PEOPLE

1. Examine your figure drawing carefully. Break up the drawing into appropriate sections which will be represented by different fabrics. Next examine each section again to make sure the shape will be possible to turn inside out. Further divide the figure if curves are too extreme. (See drawing of Encie on page 82.)

2. Place lightweight interfacing over each drawn shape and trace its outline onto the interfacing. Allow at least 1/2" between sections.

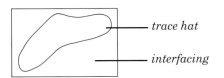

trace hat

interfacing

3. After cutting these shapes apart, pin each one to the right side of the appropriate fabric chosen for that segment.

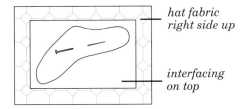

hat fabric right side up

interfacing on top

4. Sew completely along the drawn line with very tiny stitches. Trim to approximately 1/8" from the seam line.

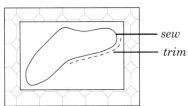

sew

trim

5. Cut a tiny slit in the interfacing and carefully turn the shape inside out.

6. Iron after making sure all the edges are completely turned and smooth.

7. Assemble all the "body parts" and attach them to each other with very tiny hand stitches.

8. Attach each figure to the quilt by using hand applique techniques.

NOTE: There is no limit to the extra embellishments that can be added to your figures. Use your imagination and dig into that box with tiny pieces of lace, ribbon, beads and buttons.

HAIR: I have used a fabric featuring a wide variety of cats (gold, white, black and gray) to represent the hair on my Victorian ladies.

Close-up from the Ball Quilt on page 29

84

WONDER-UNDER PEOPLE

1. Examine your drawing and separate into sections.

2. Turn your paper with the drawing to the back side and retrace the lines. Tape the drawing to a window if it is difficult to see through it. This back side will be used as a model for tracing onto the paper side of the Wonder-Under as the front view will produce a reversed image.

3. Trace each individual section onto the Wonder-Under and cut it out leaving at least a 1/2" border around the penciled shape.

4. Iron this shape to the wrong side of the appropriate fabric. Cut out on the pencil line and remove the paper backing.

(Where shapes touch each other you may need to allow some extra fabric so that body segments might overlap and be attached with the iron. Example: The head of a person might be elongated to extend under a hat as well as the chest.)

5. Assemble all the separate pieces on top of a larger sheet of the backing paper from Wonder-Under and carefully touch these with the iron fusing them into a whole person. This fabric figure should still have traces of the fusible webbing on the back.

6. Attach the figure by positioning it on the quilt and ironing over it. To avoid loosing a "friend" firmly secure all the people with tiny hand stitches and coordinating thread.

Close-up from the "Russell Inn Quilt" on page 13

"Victorian Homes"
(1983) - 64" x 54"
author

South Reach Road

Part Four
LOG CABINS

The Log Cabin - Folk Art Of The Past

Simply designed and solidly built, the log cabin served our early ancestors well and quickly became a part of American legend. It's image evoked a strong and courageous pioneer spirit that was used as a political tool from 1829, when Andrew Jackson was elected President, until the election of Abraham Lincoln, the last President to be born in a log cabin. This simple architectural structure still represents the foundation of our heritage and, like our homes, holds the history of all those individuals who came before us.

"American log cabins and houses were really expressions of folk art with roots in the dim past of the far northern forests of Scandinavia.

Each cabin had its own characteristics and character; varying widths of logs, different types of mud chinking depending on locality, and interesting and unique roof texture created by the variations in individually hand-split shingles." (pg. 19)

"Exposed to the weather of all the seasons, each building soon assumed the soft lavender-gray of weathered wood, which was complemented by the wispy green of early spring, the brilliant oranges and yellows of autumn leaves, and the bare brown of tree trunks in wintertime. The logs and shingles were still trees but in another form and the building fit appropriately into the landscape of early America, becoming a part of the rich, fruitful earth." (pg. 20)

The Log Cabin - Homes of the North American Wilderness, Alex W. Bealer and John Ellis, Barre Publishing Co., Barre, Mass. 1978-

Whether our interest in log homes is kindled by sentiment, or by an appreciation of its image as an architectural form, composed of, and blending perfectly into its surroundings, it is indeed a subject with vast appeal: just the element upon which a quilt can be designed!

"Retreat to the Cabin"
(1991) - 46" x 46"
Judith Youngman

Building A Log Cabin

In order to construct a primitive-looking log cabin, you must first discard a few of the piecing skills that you worked so hard to perfect! Since trees in the forest do not grow at the same rate or have the same diameters, the logs you cut out of brown or gray fabric, must express these irregularities. If a ruler and rotary cutter are used, your cabin will indeed have the look of a Lincoln Log kit. Although simple cardboard shapes are used for roofs, doors, and windows; logs and chinking are cut freely to better represent their natural form. When seaming logs and chinking, try not to sew as straight as you normally would and forget about that perfect 1/4" seam and following the edge of your foot. Remember, this is supposed to be primitive!

MATERIALS

1. FABRIC- 1/4 yd or less
   a. Logs - brown, dark gray - small prints
   b. Chinking - beige, tans, grays - very little texture or design
   c. Roof - dark fabric -Plaid, paisley, flowered, etc.
   d. Doors and Windows- accent type prints
   e. Sky- soft, muted prints
   f. Ground - green, brown plaid, stripe, etc.
2. Cardboard - thin (i.e. cereal box)
3. Sewing machine and sewing supplies
4. Thread to coordinate with logs, etc.
5. Spray starch or sizing

"Log Homes of the North"
(1990) - 66" x 66"
author

Log Cabins

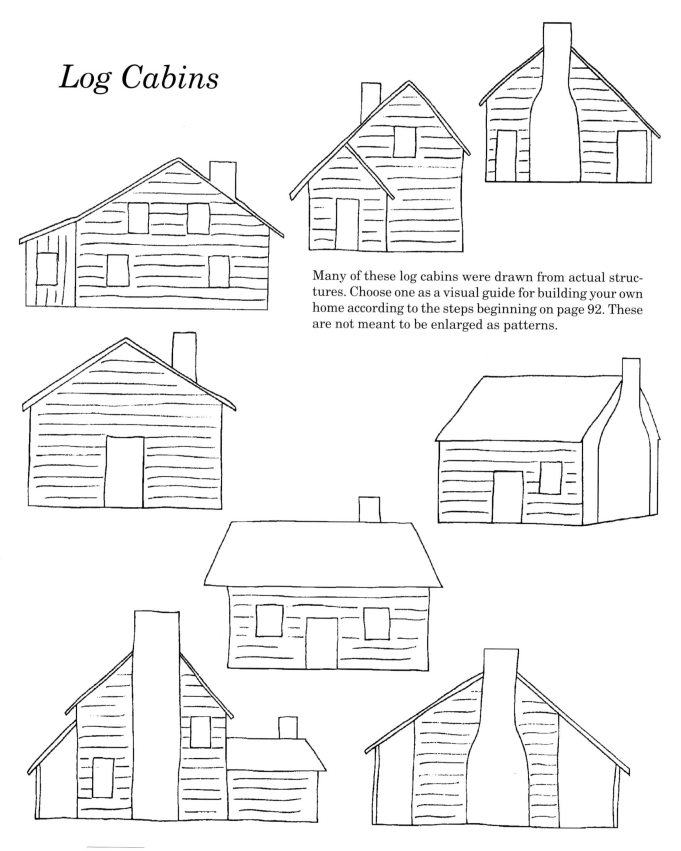

Many of these log cabins were drawn from actual structures. Choose one as a visual guide for building your own home according to the steps beginning on page 92. These are not meant to be enlarged as patterns.

"Lycoming Log Homes"
(1987) - "70 x 80" - Judith Youngman

Steps To Follow In Log Construction

1. Cut approximately 10 to 12 brown or dark gray strips for logs that are between 1" and 1 1/4" wide, and approx. 18" long. Cut freely with your scissors, do not draw any guide lines. Cut strips from your chinking fabric approx. 3/4" wide by 18" long. You will need one less than the number of logs.

2. Seam the brown and beige strips together alternating colors. Try to follow the natural curves of the strips. Trim seams where necessary and press the beige chinking toward the brown logs. Your log unit should be approx. 10" x 18". To add variety, you might seam some of the strips so that the wrong side is visible.

3. Choose a roof shape from those in the pattern inserts and make a template out of thin cardboard. Place your roof template on the wrong side of the roof fabric and cut the shape approx. 3/8" larger than the template. Spray the roof fabric with starch and iron the edges over the template. Remember to reverse the template on the wrong side of the fabric or the roof direction will be reversed.

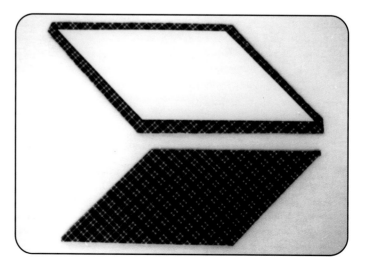

4. Place your fabric roof on top of the log unit and determine where the corners of the cabin will be. Mark these with a chalk or pencil line. If logs do not extend to the top of the gable, add more logs or use some of the excess unit that will be cut away from behind the roof.

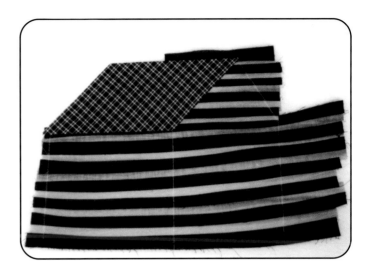

5. Cut a 1" strip of brown log fabric and iron the edges under after spraying with starch. Cover each of the cabin corners, extending the one along the gable to the roof. On the inside corner, stitch the binding along both edges. On the two outer corners, top stitch only along the inside edges. Trim the excess logs from behind both outer edges.

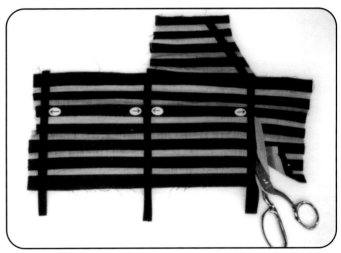

6. Cut cardboard templates to be used as shapes for windows, door, and chimney. Iron the chosen fabric for each unit over the edges of the template. The bottom edge of the door need not be turned under. When using plaids for windows, fold and iron along the lines in the plaid instead of using a template.

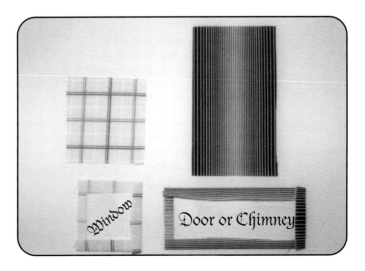

Window

Door or Chimney

7. With a straight machine stitch and matching thread, stitch the bottom edge of the roof to the cabin. Attach the windows and door by outlining their edges. Make sure the windows have a log on both top and bottom edges and the door has a log overhead. Trim away excess logs from behind the roof.

8. Place your cabin on the background (sky) fabric (18" x 22"), slip the chimney under the roof and machine stitch along the outer edge of the entire structure. The excess log unit that was trimmed away can be used as a small addition to the cabin. The roof and corner can be formed with binding.

9. Cut the foreground (grass) fabric (6" x 22"), and with right sides together, seam the grass to the sky, catching the foundation of the cabin in the seam.

10. Your completed block can now be trimmed to the size desired.

SUMMARY

These instructions are very basic and should be used as a guide to construct your first log home. As you work, you may discover other tricks that will create the effect you want. If you'd like to create a more realistic log structure, slice the original log unit where the inside corner will be formed. Adjust the units so that logs coming to the corner will meet with the chinking strip, giving the illusion of one log resting on the other. The corner can then be covered with binding as in the "Russell Inn" quilt. In that quilt the one log unit was slanted to give the illusion of depth.

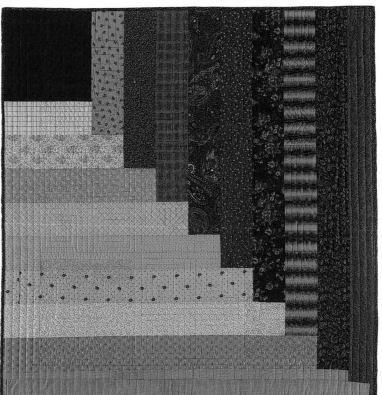

Back view of the quilt "Log Homes of the North" featuring 6" wide strips sewn in a traditional log cabin design.

SUPPLY SOURCES:

Calico Treasures - 721 Hepburn St., Williamsport, PA 17701 - (717) 326-6139
>Unusual fabrics for landscapes and architecture as well as supplies and books mentioned in this book. Send SASE for a complete list.

Pro Chemical & Dye Inc. - P.O. Box 14, Somerset, MA 02726 - (508) 676-3838
>Supplies for fabric dying and painting.

Skydyes - 83 Richmond Lane, West Hartford, CT 06117 - (203) 232-1429
>Hand-painted cottons and silks for landscapes.

ADDITIONAL READING:

Antiquity Reprints - Box 370, Rockville Centre, NY 11571, *Modern American Dwellings - 1897, Shoppell's Modern Houses - 1887* and *Houses & Cottages - 1893*

Hargrave, Harriette, *Heirloom Machine Quilting* - C & T Publishing, Lafayette CA 94549-1990

History of Lycoming County, PA, Published by D. J. Stewart - Press of J. B. Lippincott Co. - 1876/reprinted 1975

Junior League of Williamsport, Inc., *The West Fourth Street Story* - 1975, and *Homes and Heritage of the West Branch Valley* - 1968, Grit Publishing Co., Williamsport, PA
Both are available at the Lycoming County Historical Museum.

Larson, Morris, Piper, *Williamsport,* Windsor Publications, Inc., Woodland Hills CA

Naversen, Kenneth, *East Coast Victorians: Castles and Cottages,* Beautiful America Pub. Co., P.O. Box 646, Wilsonville OR 97070-1990

Pomada & Larsen, *Daughters of Painted Ladies,* E. P. Dutton, 2 Park Avenue, NY, NY 10016

Books by Dover Publications, Inc., 31 East 2nd St., Mineola, NY 11501

>Blum, Stella, F*ashions and Costumes from Godey's Lady's Book*
>Johnston, Susan, *Fashion Paper Dolls from "Godley's Lady's Book" 1840 - 1854*
>Menton, Theodore, *Victorian Fashion Paper Dolls from Harper's Bazaar, 1867 - 1898*
>Mitchell Co., *Men's Fashion Illustrations from the Turn of the Century*
>Smith, A. G., *The American House: Styles of Architecture, Coloring Book*

PLACES TO VISIT AND LEARN MORE ABOUT THE PAST:

James Brown Library - 19 E. 4th Street, Williamsport, PA 17701 - (717) 326-0536

Lycoming County Historical Museum - 858 West 4th Street, Williamsport PA 17701 - (717) 326-3326

The Peter Herdic House Restaurant - 407 W. 4th Street, Williamsport, PA 17701 - (717) 322-0165
>Winner of 1984 Award - Best Historical Restoration in PA.